D0495556

the teaching
of ecumenics

the teaching of ecumenics

Edited by Samuel Amirtham
and Cyris H.S. Moon

WCC Publications, Geneva

Cover design: Rob Lucas

ISBN 2-8254-0907-3

© 1987 WCC Publications, World Council of Churches,
150, route de Ferney, 1211 Geneva 20, Switzerland

Printed in Switzerland

Table of Contents

Preface

This book comes out of a workshop on the teaching of ecumenics which was held at the Ecumenical Institute, Bossey, Switzerland, 1-11 July 1986. The plans for this workshop date back to the Vancouver Assembly, 1983, where such a suggestion was first made at a meeting of theological educators. The Ecumenical Institute and the Programme on Theological Education of the World Council of Churches have organized many programmes and courses to train ecumenical leaders, lay people, pastors and theological students, but this was the first time that persons responsible for *teaching* ecumenics were brought together from many parts of the world.

Although there exist networks in certain regions and at world level which enable teachers of ecumenics to meet, their activities are mainly limited to ecumenical research or to assist churches in dealing with ecumenical issues, and are less related to the specific task of teaching *ecumenics* in theological faculties and schools. We discovered that teachers of ecumenics are still "rare birds" in this context, and it is not often recognized that in their own particular discipline and responsibility in theological faculties they have a vital role in the life and mission of the church.

The purpose of teaching ecumenism is twofold. First, to do so on its own merit as a discipline, to pursue research on what has divided the churches in the past, the current situation in interchurch negotiations and the contemporary issues facing the ecumenical movement. Secondly, to bring in the ecumenical perspective, the unity of church and unity of humankind, in all the disciplines and the totality of the teaching and learning experience. No church or school can afford to do theology in isolation.

Therefore, the participants at this workshop were not only teachers of ecumenics but also scholars in other disciplines such as scripture, church history, social ethics and systematics. The choice of the themes to be dealt with in depth was partly determined by the participants. Subjects like, for example, mission were left out, in the hope that these might be taken up separately at a future date.

This publication is intended to be a modest handbook, providing some directions and perspectives. The bibliography is very limited, and yet we thought it good to provide this for the benefit of schools which may not have elaborate library facilities. The course outlines are meant to be samples and not models.

The workshop itself was organized jointly by two sub-units of the WCC — the Ecumenical Institute (Bossey) and the Programme on Theological Education (PTE) — in cooperation with the Irish School of Ecumenics (ISE), Dublin, and the Washington

Institute of Ecumenics (WIE). We are grateful to Dr Robin Boyd, director of ISE, and Dr Dan Martensen of WIE for their valuable help in planning and holding this workshop. We should also express our thanks to Mr Dietrich Werner and Ms Margaret Koch for their help in the publication of the book.

We hope that this book will contribute to greater interest in the teaching of ecumenics and motivate theological teachers and students to take this field of theological study more seriously and imaginatively.

SAM AMIRTHAM, Director, PTE
ADRIAAN GEENSE, Director, Ecumenical Institute, Bossey

Introduction

Those of us who produced the material in this book hope that the text will be considered by theological educators to be a gentle but firm nudge from colleagues as well as a useful educational resource. We consider this book to be a nudge because we are convinced that academia needs to move more in the direction of the oikoumene in both theory and practice; we see it as a resource because we acknowledge that the space between academia, particularly theological education, and the emerging field of ecumenics is wide and in need of being bridged. Some comments about these two purposes are in order.

Many reasons for the gap between academia and the oikoumene might be cited. One could point to the elitist character of ecumenical work as such, a process which has for decades lifted theologians from their everyday contexts of ministry and parachuted them into various ecumenical fields of engagement; this often results in no measurable effects back home. Too, one could note the difficulty ecumenically committed teachers of theology have in fitting the messy interdisciplinary configuration of resources produced by the modern ecumenical movement into the relatively neat vertical categories of theological disciplines and departments.

The traditional encyclopedia of theological seminary concerns tends to more than fill the available space in a given curriculum, as most curricula are presently organized. Ecumenics as a self-conscious field of enquiry sits uneasily on the periphery of late twentieth-century Christian theological education. People committed to the teaching of ecumenics experience along with the uneasiness a sense of urgency, urgency related to the crying need for maintaining a corporate ecumenical memory. After nearly seventy years of organized ecumenical effort, we have no systematic means of transmitting experience, knowledge and vision generated in those decades.

Our experience as teachers of ecumenics and proponents of ecumenism reflects the tensions inherent in the ecumenical movement itself. Interaction among us, we who have been engaged in this project, has made that fact powerfully and sometimes painfully clear. There are differences among us which have to do with our individual and corporate (ecclesiastical) memories and with the ways in which we perceive the world. An accurate account of our work would have to acknowledge the importance of that which cannot be adequately recorded: intense feelings and sometimes anguished expressions of sisters and brothers distanced from one another by virtue of their being in the North or South, in the East or West, black or white, male or female, rich or poor.

It was often observed in our deliberations that the ecumenical enterprise, and certainly theological education, is shaped by those in power. One such expression took concrete form in some paragraphs written by Dr P. Velasques from Brazil. Comparable paragraphs could have been written by participants from Asia or Africa. It is therefore appropriate that they find a place in these introductory comments.

> Historically and theologically, the ecumenical movement is inextricably tied to mission; the two cannot be separated. The problem is not to define ecumenics so much as to determine the mission of the church today. I insist on the word "today" for two reasons. First, the gospel must speak to human needs in the context in which women and men live. Questions raised by actual human situations have been answered, adequately or otherwise, by traditional forms of mission. The so-called modern world has created modern problems. Among these, the gap between rich and poor nations and individuals has given rise to class struggle, putting one against the other around the world. The church was unable to detect the nature of this worldwide struggle, for she had for centuries been a blind leader of the blind, assuming the role of an institution justifying social injustice as "God's will". She became part of an instrument of oppression headed by "Christian rulers". Examples of this include Luther's opposition to the Peasants' Revolt, the Inquisition, Calvin's persecution of those who disagreed with him, the bloodshed which went hand-in-hand with Spanish and Portuguese colonization, Puritan witch hunts and so on. Nevertheless, oppression remains what it always was — sin. It implies destruction of human dignity and life.
>
> Secondly, the word "today" implies contextualization. It refers not only to present time, but to actual situations in which national and local churches find themselves. Mission is not immutable and supra-contextual as God is. The word of God meets men and women as they are and where they are, and so the meaning of mission changes according to the human situation. Humankind is menaced not only by nuclear destruction, but by other forms of violence, such as poverty, racism and sexism. Even in affluent countries, the church still has a responsibility towards the poor and oppressed. There is no poverty without wealth; the affluence of some means the poverty of others. Christian missionary responsibility includes recognition of guilt and responsible use of wealth.

As this statement of Dr Velasques indicates, inherent in the tension between academia and the oikoumene which emerged as the framework of our deliberations is the tension between academia and the ekklesia. The ecclesiological implications of contemporary ecumenism are as volatile as they are profound. Many unexamined questions hung suspended slightly below the surface of our conversation. Among them were: How does the self-understanding of a given church or defined community compare with the image it projects to the wider community? How does local or regional denominational self-awareness relate to the global expression of that same community of Christians? Is there an ecclesial character emerging in the common life of Christians involved in World Council work which carries the Council beyond the confines of its own basis or self-definition? These and other questions were quietly present among us, as though begging to be noticed. The answers to these types of questions, tentative though they may be, might prove to be the vehicles which will carry us down the trail some distance on this ecumenical journey. If the material in this book is any indication, the trip will require that we move very gingerly between ecclesial contextualism which may tend towards provincialism and the ecumenical ecclesial vision which sometimes tends towards imperialism.

Our experiences during the intensive training event which produced this book suggest many problems which must be further probed. One such is the ambiguity of the word "context".

What is a "context"? We speak of the "American context" as though it were a coherent entity. Yet any tourist in Washington will find within a few blocks of the White House throngs of the homeless, many of whom mentally ill, sleeping and urinating in the stairwells by night and screaming at the traffic by day.

What is a "context"? If there is a "Latin American context" how do we compare Nicaragua and Argentina? What do Indonesia and China have in common in the "Asian context"? The context of the female landless peasant in Brazil and India differs dramatically from that of the male industrial worker in each place.

How are the boundaries of a context determined: by social status, gender, economic status, ethnicity, political status, regionality, nationality or cultural-linguistic history? The final criterion just cited begs the additional question: How long does a context last? Does the present context of "Latin America" encompass the period of Iberian colonization, American interventionism, "manifest destiny" and multinational capitalist involvement? Or is the time frame of the context limited to the post-World War II so-called confrontation between communism and democracy?

Tied to this catalogue of questions is yet another. How are the transcontextual theological principles of God's truth and justice to be related to the contexts in which our ministries are to be carried out?

If the world is our parish and history is our epoch, as Troeltsch once said, our work is clearly cut out for us in the teaching of ecumenics.

In planning the Bossey event and in the development of this book we have attempted to be sensitive to the tensions among us and to the common problems we face in the ecumenical movement. Our goal has been to explore together in concrete fashion how ecumenics, with all its attending conflicts and ambiguities, might be infectiously caught and/or effectively taught. The documentary result is of two kinds, each presented in its own section of the book.

Part I is comprised of the major addresses and supplementary material, most of which was prepared ahead of time and presented at Bossey.[1]

This material reflects the individual perspective of the writer. Part II is constituted by the working group reports produced during the training event, supplemented by bibliographical material.

The purpose of Part II is to provide not only a theological point of departure but also some specific resources for teaching courses in ecumenics or components on ecumenics in more traditional courses of study. Basic ideas and building blocks for the design and construction of seminary level courses are provided.

We recognize, of course, that this study represents only a small first step in the development of resources needed to address the monumental task of teaching ecumenics. However, with it comes a very basic educational conviction, a conviction often expressed by Willem Visser 't Hooft during the last years of his life.

Often on the porch of his house during the many informal sessions he had with Geneva friends, Visser 't Hooft would say that one of the major failures of the modern ecumenical movement was its inability to perpetuate the ecumenical memory. He was undoubtedly correct. In no segment of the world's Christian population, including faculty and many professional ecumenical staff people, can one assume knowledge of the modern ecumenical movement. From this fact we can draw an important conclusion about the teaching of ecumenics, namely: unless ecumenics is taught in a self-conscious fashion it will not be taught at all.

Experience in theological consortia or other cooperative ventures in theological education clearly demonstrates that there is no automatic ecumenical gain from cross-registration among different seminaries, or even in attending a "non-denominational" or "ecumenical" theological school. This is why we speak throughout this text of "ecumenics" as a fairly self-contained field of inquiry. Ecumenics deals with a unique body of material and insight produced by the modern ecumenical movement. This insight and documentation impinges upon the classical theological disciplines but has its own integrity. More importantly, unless the quest for Christian unity and common witness and service is addressed in concerted fashion and in self-consciously defined courses of study, the ecumenical memory, to say nothing of the ecumenical vision of the future, will be lost.

We invite you to join us in the task.

DANIEL F. MARTENSEN
Washington, DC, USA
1 January 1987

NOTE

[1] These have been published in the October 1987 issue of *The Ecumenical Review*.

PART I
Selected Essays

1. Significant Events in the Ecumenical Movement

Alan D. Falconer

Introduction

One of our objectives is to provide an opportunity for sharing experiences in the teaching of ecumenics, through which each of us might be stimulated for, and encouraged in, our ecumenical work. One aspect of this sharing involves us in the exchange of information about teaching methods, course structures and the resources which are available for our common task. The experience of those of us involved in such teaching is, however, a limited one.

Each of us teaches in a specific context and with a particular constituency. Some of us are involved in adult education, others in the training of ordinands, and yet others in the training and supervision of post-graduate students. The course methods and content which each of us develops are determined by our particular situation. It is therefore important that our remarks are contextualized so that we can understand each other better and so that we can discern what can be applied to our situation and what can only be applied after major modification.

Another factor which determines our approach to the literature and concerns of the ecumenical movement is our own attitude to ecumenism. The literature of the ecumenical movement, of course, is subject, and must be subject, to the same scientific critique as any other body of literature. Is our purpose in teaching ecumenics, however, one of introducing our students to the body of literature of a contemporary ecclesiastical phenomenon? If so, then ecumenics will perhaps be one optional course in our academic programme alongside other optional courses, or may even be part of a course on the history of the contemporary church, and may even give the impression that the manifestation of church unity and ecumenical commitment is an option for the church. If, however, our attitude is that the manifestation of church unity is essential for the church, that each of us can learn from writers of other ecclesiastical traditions, and that theological, liturgical and ethical reflection is enriched by its common expression, then the literature of the ecumenical movement will pervade all the courses in our programme, and will be related to the whole body of literature studied in our academic programme. The methods, structures and resources of our courses will, therefore, be dependent upon our overall goal and attitude to the importance of church unity. While the academic or scientific approach to the ecumenical literature should not be affected by the weight we are going to give to the vision of ecumenism, the way in which we introduce ecumenical literature will be determined by the importance attached to ecumenism in our overall academic programme.

The situation, then, out of which my own reflections emerge is that of a post-graduate institution where students undertake structured courses for a degree in ecumenical studies in three areas of study: interchurch dialogue, interfaith dialogue and ethical questions with a major focus on peace issues, and in one area of which they undertake a piece of research. The students have therefore completed three years of theological study prior to commencing our degree programme. Our staff and student body are drawn from the major Christian traditions. Our institute also services some "optional courses" in ecumenism in Roman Catholic seminaries, and runs adult education courses, programmes and events on ecumenical themes throughout Ireland. The way in which the literature of the ecumenical movement is used, and the resources employed in each of these situations, are of course determined by the particular theme to be studied and by the background of the participants themselves.

In the programme of interchurch dialogue which treats the history and literature of the ecumenical movement most explicitly, there are five courses where we seek:

1) to lay a biblical and theological foundation for the vision of ecumenism and to introduce the student to the different ways that vision has been pursued — councils, Christian world communions, church unions, local ecumenism at parish level, etc.;

2) to explore in one topic, viz. the eucharist, the different methodologies and results of the international bilateral and multilateral agreements;

3) to examine the concept of "faith" and "theology", and to ask whether there can be an ecumenical way of doing theology;

4) to explore the concept of justification by faith and thus reconcile different memories of the same event, drawing on some contemporary ecumenical agreements;

5) to try from our respective traditions to elaborate a theology of ministry (including the Petrine ministry).

All our students are required to take the first two of these courses, so that at the very least each student should complete his or her course with a theologically based vision of ecumenism, a knowledge of the different models of church unity, and of the contemporary international agreements and their methodologies. They should also have acquired the technique of reading and understanding reports!

This then is the framework for my own work and for my remarks on significant events in the ecumenical movement. My major concern is to lay a foundation for the theology of ecumenism, and the significant events of the ecumenical movement are treated in that framework. I am, therefore, approaching these events primarily as a theologian rather than as a historian, even although I may employ the methods of historical criticism in trying to explore the meaning and significance of the events concerned. Along with our students I also have to try to discern the meaning of the ecumenical events studies — be these the Second Vatican Council, WCC Assemblies or the meetings of Faith and Order — since I have not personally attended any of these events. In approaching these ecumenical events, then, I am largely dependent on the literature emanating from and surrounding them, supplemented by the occasional "eye-witness" account!

Although the focus of this paper is on ways in which the significant events in the ecumenical movement might be taught, I would like to examine the importance of these events for an understanding of the ecumenical movement. Why is it necessary to examine the specific literature of the ecumenical movement at all?

The significance of events for an understanding of the ecumenical movement

In his *The Book of Laughter and Forgetting,* the Czechoslovakian novelist Milan Kundera offers a series of reflections on the importance of memory as the root from which the self-understanding of their identities by individuals and groups emerges. In one of the essays in the book, he analyzes the writing of Franz Kafka and comments:

> Prague in his novels is a city without memory. It has even forgotten its name. Nobody there remembers anything, nobody recalls anything... No song is capable of uniting the city's present with its past by recalling the moment of its birth.
> Time in Kafka's novel is the time of a humanity that has lost its continuity with humanity, of a humanity that no longer knows anything nor remembers anything, that lives in nameless cities with nameless streets or streets different from the ones they had yesterday, because a name means continuity with the past and people without a past are people without a name. [1]

In his essays, Kundera explores this theme in relation to the way in which an attempt has been made by the state authorities to change the awareness of the identity of the Czech people since the end of the Second World War. An attempt has been made to erase the nation's memory, and through this the identity of the people has been eroded. As Kundera notes when he quotes his friend Milan Hubl approvingly: "The first step in liquidating a people is to erase its memory."[2]

The culture, traditions, songs, religious commitment, political ideals embodied above all in the literature and poetry of the community are important vehicles communicating and challenging the identity of the society. The awareness of the history of the community highlights the struggles, ideals and mistakes made by and in relation to the community. The cohesiveness and sense of direction of the community is nourished by its memories.

Through the exploration of its memories, then, a community comes to a renewed awareness of its identity. Through an examination of its history, the identity of a community also becomes apparent to those who have not taken part in its past, thus enabling them to understand the community better, and to be confronted by its perspectives and values.

The need for what he terms a "common memory" of the ecumenical movement has been stressed recently in an important paper by José Miguez Bonino. By emphasizing the need for the ecumenical movement to articulate and appropriate its past, Bonino is suggesting that the ecumenical movement will be able to act more cohesively, and the identity or vision of ecumenism will become more apparent to those who have not yet committed themselves to it. He writes:

> The modern ecumenical movement has run for almost one century. The WCC is close to its fortieth anniversary. It is not such a long history, but it is already too long for us to rely on a *spontaneous* living memory. How, then, to "rememorate", to make the past present and effective in our daily work? There have been changes but also continuities and "metamorphosis" in this history. For a body like the WCC to maintain an organic and not merely an institutional continuity, it needs constantly to re-read and re-live its common past. [3]

5

Such an attempt to "rememorate" or to appropriate the significant events of the ecumenical movement is seen to be essential if the ecumenical movement is to grow, and if the vision, albeit a vision in process of modification, is to develop and become manifest.

But how do we decide which events are significant? Is it that the more representative an event geographically and confessionally in terms of the world church is, the more significant the event becomes? Or is an event the more or less significant the more it adheres to *my* general conception of the ecumenical issue or vision in question? Does an event become significant because it marks a complete discontinuity with what has gone before, or does the significance arise because the event clarifies and sums up all that has gone before? How do we discern the significance of events?

On discerning the significance of events

In exploring this theme, an analogy from the European musical tradition may help to illumine our thinking. In taking such a musical analogy, I am aware that it derives from a particularly European cultural tradition and thus is not universal. Each of us is to a great extent conditioned by our own cultural traditions, just as the expressions we use in our theologies are drawn from our own cultural milieu. Such a musical analogy is merely an illustration. The same principles can be elicited from other models. Indeed it may be that these same principles could be better expressed by other models drawn from other musical and cultural traditions. However, the anticipated effect of a performance in the European cultural musical tradition is that the listener also becomes drawn into or absorbed into the movement and colour of the composition. While this analogy, therefore, is limited by its evident cultural limitation, it has the advantage of offering a participatory model and of conveying the sense that the "listener" is drawn into the very dynamics and dynamism of the work itself, just as the student should be drawn into the dynamics and dynamism of the ecumenical movement through the study of the material.

The classical tradition of symphonic writing as exemplified by Mozart and the early works of Beethoven presents in each movement of the symphony connected thematic material in more or less orderly fashion which leads to the full flowering of the theme. The theme is then examined and developed either in its elemental or decorative aspects. After this development, the theme is recapitulated in the same sequence and much the same fashion as in its original statement. In this classical form there is nothing superfluous; everything is intimately and explicitly connected to the main theme. The form is self-contained.

The second symphonic form which I wish to introduce is the development of this classical form by the Romantics as exemplified in the writings of Brahms and Tchaikovsky. The Romantics attempted to provide a thread of unity existing from movement to movement, either through rhythm or through the repetition of thematic material. In this romantic form, it is the thread that runs all through the work which provides the cohesiveness. Whatever does not directly concern this thread is less significant overall, no matter how effective in its original setting. What is significant is how the different movements contribute to the development of the main theme, and the way in which that main theme is transformed as it progresses from movement to movement.

The final symphonic form for our consideration is that which is evident in the writing of the Finnish composer, Jean Sibelius. His symphonies as a whole are built on a mosaic pattern, which basically presents a mass of seemingly unrelated or even abrupt theme-fragments, as if he simply set down musical ideas as they came to him, some of which seem to lead nowhere. As Donald Grout notes in his *A History of Western Music:*

> His originality consists partly in the free use he makes of familiar chords, partly in his orchestration (emphasizing low registers and unmixed colours), but above all in the nature of his themes, his technique of thematic development, and his treatment of form. Instead of full periodic melodies, a theme may be built of short motives that, first sounded separately, gradually coalesce into a complete entity (as in the third movement of the Fourth Symphony). Motives from one theme may be transferred to another, or themes dissolved and their motives recombined in such a way that the original theme is gradually transformed by the replacing of its motivic units one by one until a new structure results (first movement of the Third Symphony). [4]

These three types of symphonic form, without trying to press the analogy too far, provide different models for approaching and discerning the significance of events.

The "classical" form suggests an approach which examines an event itself, and is primarily concerned with stimulating interest in that event alone. Thus in communicating the main motifs and dynamic tensions of the WCC Assembly at Vancouver, an account of the event which was Vancouver is given to stimulate interest in, and to show the range of concerns of, the contemporary ecumenical movement. The significance of the event which is made the object of the exercise is seen, then, in terms of its importance for the contemporary church, of its impact on the people attending, of its range of concerns, and of its specific pronouncements. Such an examination of an Assembly, for example, may further demonstrate how the churches of different confessional traditions can take decisions together on theological questions and ethical issues, and how the issues of brokenness in our world impinge on the life and reflections of Christians throughout the world. The "classical" form therefore concentrates on one event exploring all the facets of that event, and noting its impact on the participants. [5]

The second form in our analogy — the "romantic" — suggests that an event is significant insofar as it contributes to a larger development. The event, or aspects of the event, are explored and their significance assessed in the light of what has gone before, and in its impact on later developments. An example of this might be seen in terms of the Lund Faith and Order conference with the two Principles and with the ecclesiology which emerged at the conference. Prior to the Lund conference, a comparative method of doing theology had been operative. Representatives of different churches described their theological understanding of a given topic, e.g. eucharist, after which the common elements from the presentations were affirmed, and the divergences noted as items for further exploration. At the Lund Faith and Order conference a new methodology emerged when it was suggested that the theologians from different Christian traditions should attempt to articulate a common theology on specific questions. Parallel to this methodological development, the conference also affirmed that the churches should do everything together except those things which deep differences of conviction prevented their so doing. The ecclesiology which underpinned those changes was that the church is a pilgrim people, which is striving constantly to articulate its theology, learning as it journeys, and not constrained by the

7

theological statements of the past nor the ecclesiastical structures and ethical positions adopted in different circumstances and ages. The "classical" form of examining the Lund conference would be to explore these themes and their relationship to each other, through an examination of the reports and the thinking of the participants who made the proposals and discussed them. While such an investigation in this "classical" form of the Lund conference can lead to an appreciation of the dynamics and perspectives of Lund, what makes Lund "significant" is its continuity and discontinuity with previous Faith and Order conferences, and its importance in charting the methodology and agenda for future Faith and Order work. The significance of the Lund Faith and Order conference and other such events becomes apparent in its relation to the wider work of Faith and Order and the forms of interchurch dialogue. In this way, the Lund conference and other events demonstrate their significance when the "romantic" form is employed.[6]

It is, however, the analogy with the symphonic writing of Jean Sibelius which provides the most demanding exploration of ecumenical events. It is not enough, I think, simply to trace an element in the contemporary ecumenical movement. The real significance of any ecumenical event is the way in which it helps to illumine the vision of ecumenism, or challenges the current practices and theologies of the churches-in-isolation, and helps the churches to make more manifest the unity of Christians and their communities. Of course, it is not simply that the theology and practice developed in the ecumenical movement challenges the contemporary churches-in-isolation, the theology and practices of the churches-in-dialogue are also subject to critique in the light of the gospel. The significance of the event is, therefore, found in relation to the way that it is illumined by or illumines the gospel. Any one event, therefore, is significant in its relation to the theological vision of the unity of Christians and their communities. By placing ecumenical events in this context, then, their significance emerges through their contribution to the total vision of the unity of the church for the sake of the unity of humankind. It is largely by placing "significant events", as for example WCC Assemblies and Vatican II, in this context that one is led to a greater commitment to ecumenism. However, the significance of an event, in the light of this "type", lies in its relation to the overall theme, and its significance only becomes apparent in the light of that total statement of the theme, in the same way as is evident in a symphony of Sibelius, where the significance of a phrase, or a half-formed idea which in its place in the ordering of the work seems to lead nowhere, becomes apparent in the full flowering of the theme which is the climax of the work.

At this point, perhaps, a fourth example from the Western musical tradition should be given, viz. the "unfinished symphony", though not so much in the Schubertian style as in that of Sibelius! Since the churches' quest for unity is still in process, the student is being invited to enter the dynamics and dynamism of a movement which he or she is to take part in developing, transforming what has gone before in the light of changed interchurch relations, contemporary theological insights and the concrete tensions and opportunities of the world situation.

It may well be that the three "types" I have elaborated — and it must be stressed again that the musical analogy cannot be pushed too far — can themselves be seen as a process of development in academic study, just as they are in the history of musical development. The circumstances of our situation will, however, undoubtedly determine whether or not it is possible to conduct a course in the "classical", "romantic" and "Sibelius" mode, or employ all three in a process of development. However, the significance of the event under discussion is evident only in the light of the gospel and the total ecumenical vision. Seemingly insignificant details become keys to understanding that vision, whereas often that which was thought to be of great significance is seen to be of less importance.

With all three types, ecumenical literature must be examined so that the event itself — be that a WCC Assembly, a bilateral dialogue, a Faith and Order report, the Programme to Combat Racism or the Vatican Council — is allowed to speak for itself. Any such event needs to be analyzed so that it can be understood on its own terms. In trying to suggest guidelines for this process, I have drawn up the following notes for the reading of reports, which I give to students.

Some guidelines for reading the reports of "Significant Events"

1. *Examine the list of participants.* Dialogue is an "experience" of the individual participants. Therefore, examine:
a) who they are, in terms of their "disciplines", cultures, experiences of life;
b) what traditions are represented;
c) what previous work has been done by them as individuals on the theme under discussion.
All these affect the insights they bring to the dialogue.

2. *Examine the preparatory documents and the draft schema.* Dialogue is a process. Therefore examine the discussion documents by the various participants, and the "feed in" by other groups. Cf. the contribution of the Les Dombes agreement when submitted as one response to the first draft which eventually led to the eucharist statement on BEM.

These lead to:

3. *Draft schema.* Here one examines the journey which the commission has made. What they have decided to add, or exclude from their previous draft: cf. the inclusion of *subsistit* in the Vatican II Decree on Ecumenism, and the exclusion of *est*.

4. *Examine the previous relations between the communions represented in the interchurch dialogue.* This pre-history will often determine the subjects for, and methodology of, the dialogue. Cf. ARCIC and the influence of the Wake-Girardin correspondence; the Oxford movement; the Lord Halifax-Portal conversations 1892-1896; and the Malines conversations of 1922-1926.

5. *Note the time of the meeting.* What might impinge on the awareness of the delegates, e.g. WCC Nairobi Assembly (1975). The reports, particularly Section 1, contain allusions to the theology of Bonhoeffer (30th anniversary of his execution), and to the kingdom of God (50th anniversary of the Stockholm Life and Work conference on this theme).

The situation in the world also needs to be examined as it impinges on the delegates. Cf. the importance of the "Cold War" at the Amsterdam Assembly (1948) especially in respect of the exchanges between John Foster Dulles and Josef Hromadka.

6. *Compare the report with others on the same subject.* Why does the report under review treat this topic which others have not felt it necessary to examine? Does this report treat the subject in a different way and why?

Note also the cross-fertilization which might be taking place between reports on the same subject.

7. *Note the current writings on the subject under discussion.* These obviously influence the thinking of the participants.

As one applies guidelines such as these, then the events are themselves allowed to address us. The significance of the event or report studied, however, even though such guidelines are followed for the interpretation of the event, emerges more fully in relation to other such events, and the vision of the unity of the church for the sake of humankind.

Teaching "significant events" — some illustrations

For the most part, in teaching courses on ecumenical themes, our institute has a practice of asking students to undertake some prior reading which will give them a general orientation in the field of study before the course itself begins. In preparation, therefore, for the course on the theological foundations of ecumenism, students are required to read a history of the ecumenical movement,[7] a brief account of the theological perspectives of ecumenism,[8] and an account of the structure, concerns and history of the WCC.[9] From this, it is hoped that the student will have a sense of the major concerns and perspectives of the ecumenical movement, so that we can then concentrate on trying to lay a theological foundation for ecumenism.

In exploring a theological framework for ecumenism attention is paid to the theme of unity and oneness in the Bible, and to the perception and experience of oneness enunciated by the early Christians. A fundamental aspect of that oneness was their awareness that they as a community were to live "as" (*kathos*) God is one — manifesting in their living the oneness of the Godhead. Thus to explore the unity of the church involves exploring the oneness of God, which is to be source and paradigm for the oneness of the church. The church is a community defined by, and in its relation to God. The church is also a community which lives this relationship as it seeks to confess its faith in God, to celebrate the presence of God in worship, and to live a life-style consonant with the understanding of God and of God-in-relation-to-humankind.[10]

In the light of this theological foundation, the reports of the "significant events" of the ecumenical movement are then explored in relation to their enunciation of the unity of the church and their reasons for stressing the importance of the manifestation of church unity. Thus the "significant events" are subjected to the analysis of the students in the light of this theological foundation, and simultaneously the events are perceived as "significant" in the light of these perspectives — the methodological analogy is that of the Sibelius type enunciated above.

In our examination of the ecclesiology, a different approach to the reports of the "significant events" is taken. As you will have perceived, I described the church in relation to God and in terms of the three marks of the church enunciated by the fathers of the Reformed tradition, viz. the church is the community of word, sacrament and discipline. In respect of each of these three "marks" of the church, we explore together the major ecumenical programme on that mark. Thus in exploring the nature of the church as confessing community, after examining the nature and limits of confessions of faith, we explore the Faith and Order programme relating to confessing the faith today which encouraged churches in their local situation to confess the faith — a programme which has now developed into the study "Towards a Common Confession of the One Apostolic Faith". Similarly with the church as eucharistic community, we explore the concept of eucharistic ecclesiology, and examine BEM and the "renewal of community" programmes. For the church as the community of discipline or discipleship we look at a specific ethical programme, normally the human rights work of the churches and the WCC. In each of these cases it is possible to examine the programmes mentioned as studies in their own right. By placing our reflections in the context of an examination of the nature of the church, however, the student perceives that the ecumenical movement is addressing the churches at the centre of their being, and that the specific programmes of the ecumenical movement are helping the church to be the church. The student is therefore able to perceive that the study of "significant events" can not only be interesting, but that the events have also immense significance for the church if it is to be true to its nature. While I have developed this material in a course trying to establish a theological foundation for ecumenism, it seems to me that there is no reason why the same material could not be used in the same way in any course on ecclesiology. Support for this may be found in the recent book by Anton Houtepen, *People of God: a Plea for the Church*, which adopts this approach, while the earlier work by W.A. Visser 't Hooft, *The Pressure of Our Common Calling*, also employs the same perspectives. [11]

In the course which I have been elaborating up to this point the major purpose has been to develop a theology of ecumenism which will motivate students to see that the ecumenical movement is not an option for the church but is the attempt to manifest the core of the gospel through a community which places at its centre the confession of God's grace and care for humankind (the term *missio Dei* in various ecumenical documents seeks to affirm this also), the celebration of God's presence, and the discipleship which is the living response to the activity of God. Through this the reports of "significant events" are seen to acquire their significance by empowering the church to be, and thus freeing the churches from their isolation and drawing them towards each other in fellowship. It is hoped that through this the student will appropriate the "significant events" and make them their own.

In the rest of this course, we look at specific attempts and models to manifest that oneness, examining the relevant literature and commentaries, and asking whether the model under inspection takes seriously enough the theological and ecclesiological foundation which has been laid.

In the context of discussing conciliar fellowship, the first explicit attempt is made to explore a facet of the Second Vatican Council. The question is posed as to whether the Roman Catholic Church can or should become a member of the World Council of Churches. To answer this, the student is encouraged to read the biography of Pope John XXIII by Peter Hebblethwaite, the recently published book *Vatican II by Those Who Were There*, edited by Alberic Stacpoole, the *Decree on Ecumenism* and the subsequent directory, the commentaries on the *Decree*, and the studies on the question of Roman Catholic membership of the WCC published in *The Ecumenical Review* and in booklet form in the United States. Of course, to answer this question it is necessary also to explore the nature of the WCC through an examination of the Toronto Statement, and the discussion since then on the ecclesiological significance of the WCC. Finally the question is addressed by taking into account the history of Vatican-WCC relations and the operational difficulties experienced by the Joint Working Group. [12] In elucidating this particular session of the course — a question which is also set as an essay topic for the students — I have been at pains to give indications as to how the "significant event" of the Second Vatican Council is treated. The attempt is made to let the Council itself speak, through studying the dynamics of the Council's own discussions, noting the dramatic change in ecumenical relations from all that had happened previously, and exploring the significance of this event through an assessment of how far the Roman Catholic Church has been enabled to accept the ecclesial nature of other churches, and to enter into fellowship at the local level with other churches.

The final session of this course is one where I use photo language material and techniques to encourage the students to talk about their view of the vision of ecumenism, thus assessing their appropriation of the material and their commitment to shaping the developing "symphonic themes".

As a further recommendation to our students, it is suggested that they might read the biography or autobiography of a prominent ecumenist — I call this "bedtime reading"! — to discern what motivated the persons ecumenically to the extent that they devoted their life to the ecumenical vision. For their own personal meditation, the students are also introduced to the daily reading Bible notes of the International Bible Reading Fellowship *Word for the World* which link biblical reflection with important passages from ecumenical reports, and to the books of Hans-Ruedi Weber – *Immanuel* and *On a Friday Noon* – which introduce the reader to the diversity and richness of Christian art and literature, thus reasserting how much we learn from each other in our common pilgrimage. [13]

The account of this mode of encountering the ecumenical literature suggests the model posed by the musical analogy with Sibelius. As a framework it enables the student to encounter ecumenical literature and to treat it seriously while being motivated also to take the ecumenical vision seriously, and to appropriate the "significant events".

As a second example, I take a course which adopts the "romantic" typology. In a course on eucharist and eucharist sharing, we basically analyze, in respect of both the methodology adopted and the content, three of the current agreements on the eucharist — ARCIC, the Reformed-Roman Catholic agreement and BEM. These texts are explored thoroughly after an introduction to the course which presents through a commentary on, and examination of, the liturgical schema of different churches, the contemporary convergence on the structure, text and understanding of the eucharistic rite. Such an account is, of course, reinforced for the students by their participation in the worship of other churches in their "fieldwork exercises".

When we noted the guidelines for reading reports earlier I briefly hinted at the direction taken in our study of the background to ARCIC from the Archbishop Wake-Girardin correspondence to the present day. That correspondence is decisive for an understanding of ARCIC since it establishes firmly a distinction between fundamentals and non-fundamentals in theology, the fact of diversity in theological and liturgical expression, and the theological problem to be faced in terms of the sacrifice of Christ, and the presence of Christ in the eucharist. This of course is one instance where a complete ecumenical failure has been determinative for later rapprochement! The ARCIC material is explored, as are the reactions and responses of the churches and groups within the churches to it, e.g. the Evangelicals, and attention is drawn to the materials developed as aids to discussing ARCIC in parishes.

A similar procedure is followed in the other reports studied. Thus in relation to BEM, the Faith and Order discussions on the eucharist from Lausanne 1927 to the current time are explored, noting the impact of the Lund method, and of the work of Max Thurian, from his writing on *Eucharistic Memorial* to his drafting of the Lima Liturgy. When considering BEM we also look at the different ways in which different churches have participated in the process which led to the final statement. While the 1967 and subsequent drafts and the final reports have been sent to presbyteries and congregations for discussion and response in the Reformed churches, other churches have responded by statements from hierarchies adopted after the recommendation of specialized groups. Through this an appreciation of the process of shaping ecumenical texts and of "reception" becomes apparent, thus leading to an appreciation of the limits and possibilities for the future involvement of the student in the process of the interchurch theological dialogue. (Different possibilities arise in respect of the engagement in social action ecumenically.) This course on the eucharist is taught in similar forms to adult education groups and is normally completed by a celebration of the Lima Liturgy. With our degree course students, we sometimes set up working parties to write a contemporary liturgy or agreed statement as an exercise for ourselves. The ecumenical literature, then, of the "significant events" is here treated in terms of the development of a theme in line with the "romantic" typology treated above, though the importance of the topic in the light of the general vision of ecumenism has been given in the consideration of the nature of the church in another course. Through this course, the student is informed of the results of the latest ecumenical statements, is made aware of the different methodologies adopted and the reception and process of reception of the reports, and is introduced to theological and liturgical material which may be adopted and adapted for use in parishes.

In other courses, material from "significant events" — Vatican II and the different Assemblies of the WCC — is used in the attempt to construct together as staff and students a theology of justification by faith, a theological approach to ministry and the Petrine ministry and a framework for doing theology together. While the material from these events may seem incidental when used in this way, it is in fact essential to the enterprise and it is evident that once again it has largely been through the ecumenical movement that fundamental theological and ecclesiological questions for the churches have been raised.

The only occasion in which a "classical" typology as noted above is brought into operation in our teaching is when a seminar on a very recent ecumenical event is held. Thus William Lazareth recently led a seminar on the Lima Faith and Order conference, while others have presented the main themes and experiences of the Nairobi and Vancouver WCC Assemblies, and the conferences of the Catholic Conference of European Bishops. These have been stimulating occasions through which some participants seek to learn more, and through which former students are enabled to be sustained in their commitment. These do not, however, lead to the same degree of ecumenical commitment as the other "types", in our experience.[14]

When teaching this material in other institutions the basic courses outlined above are adapted, and the literature used is adapted to the level of the students concerned. After a number of years of presenting material from this literature by way of the "classical" and "romantic" typology, I felt the need to change to the "Sibelius" typology. Through the "classical" and "romantic" types it is possible to introduce people to the material of the "significant events", i.e., the literature specific to the ecumenical movement. Such material is interesting and illuminating. The students of course examine such material critically as they do in any other course in their theological studies. However, I began to realize that for too many of these students, even though they were appreciative of the courses, they were not sufficiently motivated ecumenically. It still seemed to them that ecumenism was an option. While the "significant events" could help them to expand their horizons, they did not give them enough of a sense of the vision of ecumenism. However, as the courses relating these events to the fundamental theology and mission of the church have been developing, more students have been appropriating the material and seeing it as essential that the vision of oneness become manifest.

Nearly all the material I have mentioned is related to the Faith and Order concerns of the ecumenical movement. This is because it is my task to teach theology rather than ethics or interfaith dialogue. However, I am convinced of the importance of the ethical and interfaith dimensions of ecumenism and try to convey this concern, but other colleagues teach that material. I have also omitted specific consideration of the assemblies and reports from regional councils and assemblies. The same "typology", however, occurs with respect to these. It is however important to include the material from such assemblies and gatherings in courses on ecumenics as they invite students from other geographical regions and cultural traditions to listen to the experiences of those in that situation as they struggle to proclaim and live the gospel in their context. I am also convinced that the major problems to be overcome in the attempt to make manifest the oneness of the church are the so-called "non-theological" factors, and they need to be examined through interdisciplinary work with the social sciences.

In this paper I have attempted to rationalize my own teaching programmes so that discussion on the teaching of ecumenical literature can be opened up. Undoubtedly these courses have developed in an *ad hoc* way over the years. However, I hope that some perspectives on method, content and materials have helped our mutual discussions. Having had the experience as a student myself that it was the literature of the "significant ecumenical events" which stimulated me and helped me to ask fundamental theological questions, I am convinced of their value for the development of a theology which transcends confessional boundaries and which draws us into fellowship with each other to the glory of God – the Father, Son and Holy Spirit.

NOTES

[1] Trans. Michael H. Heim, Harmondsworth, UK, Penguin, 1983, p. 157.
[2] *Ibid.*, p. 159. While I am not in a position to gauge the accuracy of Kundera's perceptions in relation to Czechoslovakia, his perspectives do seem applicable to Lithuania. See my article "A Visit to the USSR", *Doctrine and Life*, 34 (10) 85, pp. 590-594.
[3] "The Concern for a Vital and Coherent Theology", report to the Executive Committee of the WCC, Kinshasa, Zaire, March 1986.
[4] London, Dent, 1980, 3rd ed., p. 665. These symphonic forms are evident also as types of structure in the writing of poets in the same period. They are exemplified also in the paintings (and possibly also the music and poetry) of Mikalojus K. Ciurlionis (1875-1911), the Lithuanian poet, painter and musician who developed a series of "sonata" form paintings where a theme is developed on three or four canvasses in some cases according to "classical" musical form, and in others according to the "romantic" or "Sibelius" types.
[5] Thus the material available for an exploration of the Vancouver Assembly would include the preparatory materials, e.g. *Images of Life*; *Issues*; *Lord of Life*; and esp. John Poulton, *The Feast of Life*, Geneva, WCC,

1982; the report of the Assembly, David Gill ed., *Gathered for Life*, Geneva, WCC, 1983; the reports by various participants, e.g. Martin Conway, *Look, Listen, Care*, London, BCC, 1984; and the video and tape cassette material issued by the WCC on the Assembly.

[6] See the Lund Faith and Order report in Lukas Vischer ed., *A Documentary History of Faith and Order 1927-1963*, St Louis, Bethany Press, 1963. The significance of the methodological change is emphasized by e.g. Kuncheria Pathil, *Models in Ecumenical Dialogue*, Bangalore, Dharmaran Publications, 1981. The Lund Principle led, amongst others, to the Nottingham Faith and Order Conference (1964) and the pledge of the British churches to try to unite by Easter day 1980, and thus indirectly led to the formation of the United Reformed Church, and to the covenant proposals in England and Wales; to the covenant of the churches in Wales; the multilateral conversations in Scotland; and to the Methodist-Presbyterian shared church and ministry schemes in Ireland — to name its impact on churches in only one very small geographical area. It is important to include consideration of the effect of the world conferences and events on the life of churches in a region as part of the study of the event itself.

[7] Either Barry Till, *The Churches Search for Unity*, Harmondsworth, Penguin, 1972, which although it is not totally accurate did include an account of the Roman Catholic Church and ecumenism; or John Matthews, *The Unity Scene,* London, BCC, 1986. Students can later be introduced to the "official" history of the ecumenical movement, and to the ecumenical movement in specific regions of the world.

[8] Either Paul Crow, *Christian Unity: Matrix for Mission*, New York, Friendship Press, 1982, or William Rusch, *Ecumenism: a Movement Toward Church Unity*, Philadelphia, Fortress, 1985.

[9] E.g. W. A. Visser't Hooft, *The Genesis and Formation of the WCC*, Geneva, WCC, 1984; or Ans van der Bent, *What in the World is the World Council of Churches?*, Geneva, WCC, 1978.

[10] For an outline of this course see my article "Theological Foundations for Ecumenism", Milltown Studies, No. 7, spring 1981, pp. 1-20.

[11] Anton Houtepen, *People of God: a Plea for the Church*, London, SCM, 1984; W. A. Visser't Hooft, *The Pressure of our Common Calling*, London, SCM, 1959.

[12] Peter Hebblethwaite, *John XXIII*, London, Chapman, 1984; A. Vorgrimler ed., *Commentaries on the Documents of Vatican II*, New York, Herder, 1965; Alberic Stacpoole ed., *Vatican II by Those Who Were There*, London, Chapman, 1986; and T. Stransky and J. Sheerin eds., *Doing the Truth in Charity*, New York, Paulist, 1982.

[13] Both published by the WCC.

[14] Bibliographic materials for teaching according to these typologies may be found in the appendix to this volume, and in the outline of group report on the teaching of "ecumenics".

2. Ecumenics as Reflections on Models of Christian Unity

Paul A. Crow, Jr

Both ecumenism (vision) and ecumenics (teaching discipline) have to do with the integrity of the church, its nature and mission, and with faithfulness to the gospel.

Ecumenics is an academic, pastoral, missional, and ecclesial discipline whose objective is to equip men and women to proclaim Christ's message of reconciliation and call the community to fulfill the mission of the Triune God and to manifest the church's unity in the whole inhabited world. Any exploration of the purpose and methodology of ecumenics raises for consideration the fundamental nature of the church and its ministry as well as the character of theological education. Ecumenics is engagement in Christian ministry in such a way as to witness to the ministry of Jesus Christ. The essence of his ministry was a life of service, sacrifice, and reconciling love. In him the word became flesh in order to reconcile all people and all creation to the Triune God. This ministry of reconciliation creates a new community which is continually built up and sent forth by the good news of the gospel. The work of the ministry of reconciliation is entrusted to all who are baptized into Christ, but especially to those persons chosen, called, and set apart for the ordained ministry. The Holy Spirit unites in a single body all those who follow Jesus Christ and sends them as witnesses into the world. Ecumenics involves critical reflection about and disciplined preparation of the whole people for this ministry of the reconciliation of all humanity. This reflection leads us to consider and critique those concepts of unity *and* models of union which bear relevant witness to the one body of Christ today.

The context of the church's witness to unity

Before we address the particular models of unity which witness to the one body of Christ, it is crucial to grasp the dynamics which mark the human situation today. The church's structures are continually being challenged, shaped and changed by the influences and structures of society. Indeed, the church can only be a sign and foretaste of God's intention for all humankind, if it is a *relevant* sign of God's uniting purpose for the world. So awareness of the contemporary world situation is critical in our particular reflections on ecclesial models. Among the transforming realities in our present world, I shall refer to three which present profound implications for the church's unity and mission, and compel us to search for this unity as the basis for world community.

16

At this historical moment, there is first a *truly global consciousness*. By this is meant that the people of the earth now live in an interconnected and interdependent world system which has never before existed. The liturgies of this global situation are economics, politics, communications, transportation, military deployment, and education. Multinational corporations use the forces of technology and commerce to shrink the distances between people and countries. Medical technology and healing can be shared instantly. Military powers can move their weapons and capacities for overkill at supersonic speeds as tensions move from continent to continent. Agronomists and weather scientists use global instruments to chart the planting and harvesting of food. Satellite television is the daily carrier of the world cup finals, papal visits, the fundamentalist preaching of entrepreneural ministers, the demands of terrorists, and other events which make people aware of their common situation. Even ecological concerns teach us we are a common family.

Increasingly persons of different, often conflictive, nations, races, and cultures are realizing they share a single atmosphere, a single source of water, the same small earth. We live under the shadow of the same bomb which gives us the means of destroying civilization and the human race. We are mutually vulnerable and bear a common fear for the future, for our families, and for the whole of human life. Whether in its positive or negative expressions this global awareness has given a new imagery for our self-understanding. Modern science and technology, says Barbara Ward, the renowned British economist, have brought the people of the world so close together in a network of communication, travel, and interdependence that "planet earth on its journey through infinity has acquired the intimacy, the fellowship, and the vulnerability of a spaceship". [1]

The dilemma of this global consciousness is clear. It can produce good or it can mastermind evil. We have become neighbours in terms of inescapable physical proximity and instant communication. Yet global awareness does not itself automatically produce a new world community. Tourist guides or overseas business partners do not necessarily become friends or neighbours. Ironically in a time of planetary communications the human race is living on the brink of ultimate destruction by famine, racial struggle, or nuclear war. The basic human question remains the same as the one the lawyer asked Jesus: "Who is my neighbour?" The church lives at the crossroads of that question, testing whether the advent of global consciousness can be translated into authentic human community.

The second reality which is shaping our new history is *pluralism*. Among the hallmarks of humanity none is more long-lasting in history or as potentially explosive today as pluralism. It has many forms — religious, cultural, or ideological — and can be described as a situation "in which various religions, philosophies, and ideological conceptions live side by side and in which none of them holds a privileged status". [2] While pluralism has long been present in human history, it has reached new heights of sensitivity and acceptance in the last quarter of the twentieth century. People have developed a sense of pride in their own culture, ethnicity, or nation — either one of which might have been eclipsed in the past by a dominant culture or ethnic identity. In this ascendency of pluralism the value of one's history is claimed positively and publicly. Diversity is accepted as creative and constructive for human relations. Pluralism is a virtue to be celebrated.

Pluralism has increasingly become a critical issue in the quest for human community. It has the potential for conflict and new alienations or for convergence and bridges of understanding. In this sense pluralism is far more than an academic issue; it is an existential matter. This fact presses upon us certain questions: How can men and women — committed to different faiths or different cultures or different political ideologies — live together in pluriform societies? In a world becoming smaller in distances and more diverse in beliefs and life-styles, are there alternatives to be found between shallow friendliness and intolerant fanaticism? What is the Christian contribution in the quest for human community in pluralistic situations? Answers to these critical questions are essential if the church is to fulfill its mission in the new world situation.[3]

Mission in such a dramatically pluralistic society brings two implications to the fore. First, if it is to witness effectively the church must accept more intentionally the pluralism in its own life as a permanent, positive attribute. The history of Christianity is rich with *de facto* diversities in theology, liturgy, spirituality, ethics, and polities, many of which until recent years suffered under the presumed dominance of one tradition. Indeed, one could define church history as the story of certain Christian institutions or theologies which built themselves as fortresses of uniformity attempting to resist, if not abolish, all others in the name of a false monolithic vision. In contrast, the modern ecumenical movement has led Christians in all traditions to confess and claim a legitimate pluralism which corresponds to the varieties of God's graces and charisms or, as Yves Congar says, to accepting pluralism as "the intrinsic value of unity".[4] Bringing this diversity into one communion is the crux of the ecumenical task. What is hopeful in this generation is that the prospects for unity are more credible because of the more openly acknowledged pluralism within the human community.

Second, mission in the new pluralism gives more importance to the partnership between Christians and persons of other faiths. Interfaith dialogue opens up those occasions when different spiritual commitments encounter each other. Such dialogue involves genuine respect for the other: it becomes a means of spiritual renewal and a way of building up community life. What is dramatically new in ecumenism and in interfaith dialogue is the recognition, esteem, and love for *the other*. In ecumenism the Roman Catholics, Orthodox, and Protestants need the others. In interfaith dialogue Christians need Muslims, Hindus, *et al.,* in the search for truth and community. Pluralism, therefore, calls for an ecumenism which spends less time and energy on the church's internal constitution and more on the larger issues of all persons and peoples. "Pluralism so understood can provide the momentum for a new united witness of the whole church of Christ in and to the whole world."[5]

The third reality which constitutes the context for the search for Christian unity is *the struggle for the survival of the human race*. This generation is confronted by planetary problems of diminishing supplies of energy and food; of conflicts of nations, cultures, races, and religions; of anarchy, injustice, and the denial of human rights; of the ominous threat of nuclear warfare and the possibility of annihilation. These apocalyptic possibilities have brought a sense of alienation, absurdity, and the immediacy of death to the peoples of the earth.

To pose the issue of human survival in this way is not to engage in doomsaying. Christians live with a theology of hope which declares that the destiny of the world is in God's hands. Justice, peace, and liberation of all people are God's gifts meant for this earth and its history. But we should never forget that God also gives freedom to us human creatures; we can accept or reject God's will in creation and redemption. We live in the presence of choices whose consequences may be terribly costly. The human race can choose life or we can choose death. As Barbara Ward says: "The plain truth is if we cannot as a human community create institutions of civilized living, our chances of carrying on the human experiment are just about nil."[6] Equally poignant, the poet W. H. Auden wrote: "We must love one another or die."

For the church the destiny of earth and the survival of the human family are far more than political or societal issues. Survival and salvation are theological issues. When Christians and other people of moral conscience are feeding and caring for the poor and destitute, trying to maintain health and a meaningful quality of life, striving for peace and justice among God's children, proclaiming Christ's reconciling love among the divided churches, they are participating in the fulfilment of spiritual and moral goals which are related to God's creation and redemption. They are living out a profoundly global, theological vision of the people of God.

The North American consultation, sponsored by the Programme on Theological Education in 1981, on "Global Solidarity in Theological Education" offered important clues for the church's role in the discovery of human community. The most powerful clue came in an address by Samuel D. Proctor, the minister of the Abyssinian Baptist Church in Harlem, a destitute section of New York City:

> Can we find a basis for a broader, deeper and more durable community that embraces our common destiny as dwellers on planet earth, that affirms our common humanity, that recognizes our possibilities as persons who have freedom, who use the subjective mood, who have a sense of "perhaps", who write poetry, build organs, fly to other planets, create options where none appear, make deserts bloom, and who stand still in quiet places to hear the voice of God?[7]

Such a vision of human community points to the vocation of the church. It calls for a church which avoids all parochial identity, lives in continuity both with the achievements of the past and the hopes for the future, and understands that its mission is to call the world to accept God's destiny. In this light ecumenism is the church's vocation to offer, through its faith and life, the basis for an inclusive and durable community whose witness is given for a frightened and endangered world.

In the last quarter of the twentieth century the church's pursuit of visible unity must take place in the midst of the three realities we have identified — globalization, pluralism, and the struggle for survival. Each has the potential for ultimate alienation or for ultimate unity. Together they surely condition and offer profound insights as to the models of Christian unity which will make the church more faithful. We now focus our attention on the struggle for faithful models.

Concepts and the shape of the church's unity

In order for the churches to advance towards their unity in Christ, it is essential to have a commonly accepted vision of the goal. What is the nature of the unity we seek? What concept of unity empowers the pilgrimage, inspires our prayers, and animates our feeble steps. What is the unity promised to the church and which will be given to us in God's time if we respond obediently to God's calling to reconciling love? These questions were assumed, even if unspoken, in the early theological reflections of the modern ecumenical movement. It was not until twenty-five years ago, however, in the context of the World Council of Churches that consensus began to unfold as to the shape of the unity to come.

The first commonly agreed-upon concept of unity was articulated at the Third Assembly of the World Council of Churches in 1961 at New Delhi. The moment was right, said the churches, to express more clearly "the nature of our common goal... the vision of the one church [which] has become the inspiration of our ecumenical endeavour". This vision they expressed in one of the longest but most crucial sentences ever written in church history:

> We believe that the unity which is both God's will
> and his gift to the church
> is being made visible
> as all in each place
> who are baptized in Jesus Christ and confess him
> as Lord and Saviour
> are brought by the Holy Spirit
> into one fully committed fellowship,
> holding the one apostolic faith,
> preaching the one gospel,
> breaking the one bread,
> joining in common prayer
> and having a corporate life reaching out
> in witness and service to all
> and who at the same time are united with the whole
> Christian fellowship in all places and all ages
> in such wise that ministry amd members are accepted by all,
> and that all can act and speak together as occasion requires
> for the tasks to which God calls his people.[8]

The New Delhi statement claims a unity that is visible and whose form is expressed "in each place" and "in all places and ages". In other words, the authentic unity of the church is both local and universal. Unity is also described as "one fully committed fellowship", a unity whose character is intense and intimate. In contrast with church-to-church competition or confessional isolation, such a visible unity portrays an intimacy of life in which the churches share deeply the good gifts of God. The signs of this intimacy are nothing less than proclaiming the one apostolic faith together, participating in common praise and prayer, celebrating the one baptism, sharing regularly in a common eucharist, mutually accepting members and ministers, sharing a corporate life which allows the church to be engaged in a common mission in the name of Christ. Beyond the fact that this vision was accepted by the WCC, it is important to realize that New Delhi's vision is substantially the same as that of the Second Vatican Council.

At the Fourth Assembly at Uppsala (1968) this view of unity was reaffirmed and exegeted more fully to emphasize visible unity as "a dynamic catholicity". Catholicity, said Uppsala, is "the opposite of all kinds of egotism and particular-ism. It is the quality by which the Church expresses the fullness, the integrity, and the totality of life in Christ."[9] True catholicity involves a quest for diversity in unity and continuity. In its witness to catholicity, the church "is bold in speaking of itself as the sign of the coming unity of [hu]mankind".[10] To achieve this vision,

Uppsala stated, two implications are required: (1) true unity and authentic models of union require a fuller understanding of the church's context, namely, a world broken and fragmented; (2) true unity is the gift of companionship with God's people who are struggling for peace and justice. A united church is therefore a universal community where people of different traditions, cultures and races are brought into "an organic and living unity in Christ". The main expression of this universality will be "a genuinely universal council" which can speak and teach for all Christians. The impact of this vision on the churches can be seen in the amazing fact that between the New Delhi (1961) and Uppsala (1968) Assemblies over twenty united churches were formed, most of which were deliberately seeking to incarnate the elements set forth in the New Delhi vision. Yet Uppsala gave a clue of an enlarged perception of the ecumenical vision. Beyond the confessional divisions between the churches, the church's visible unity is a witness to new tensions and alienations, often separating Christians within the same church or across confessional boundaries, which divide the church and humankind — the struggle for political and social justice, the search for cultural identity, the search for peace, for racial inclusiveness, and the like.

The Fifth Assembly at Nairobi (1975) reaffirmed the New Delhi statement, as expanded by Uppsala, and restated this goal of unity in new language using the imagery of "conciliar fellowship". This view was actually first drafted in 1973 by a Faith and Order consultation on "Concepts of Unity and Models of Union" at Salamanca, Spain. Our consideration requires that we quote the full text:

> The one church is to be envisioned as a conciliar fellowship of local churches which are themselves truly united. In this fellowship each church possesses, in communion with the others, the fullness of catholicity, witnesses to the same apostolic faith, and therefore recognizes the others as belonging to the same church of Christ and guided by the same Spirit. As the New Delhi Assembly pointed out, they are bound together because they have received the same baptism and share the same eucharist; they recognize each other's members and ministries. They are one in their common commitment to confess the gospel of Christ by proclamation and service to the world. To this end each church aims at maintaining sustained and sustaining relationships with her sister churches, expressed in conciliar gatherings whenever required for the fulfillment of her common calling."[11]

While these definitions of the future unity of the church have been celebrated by the churches, eventually two other dynamics are required, in my judgment, if they are to serve the actual reconciliation of these communions. (1) The commonly accepted goal will need to be "received", i.e. claimed as their goal, by the churches. (2) The unity envisioned must be expressed in particular forms or models of union. To the latter, we now turn our attention.

The vision incarnate: models of unity and union

EARLY FAITH AND ORDER DIALOGUE ON MODELS OF UNION

The ecumenical pilgrimage, by the grace of God, comes to the point when the vision must be realized. A concept of unity, with its constitutive elements, has to be manifested and experienced in the form and structure (order) of the church. This very issue was before the churches in the early days of the modern ecumenical movement, even as they reflected through a comparative methodology upon the differing views of scripture, authority, baptism, the Lord's supper, and ministry. In the midst of these early discussions and debates there was raised again and again the pervasive question of ecumenical ecclesiology, i.e. what form or order can best express the unity God wills for the church?

In the 1920 Faith and Order's Continuation Committee, representatives from 40 countries and 17 churches met in Geneva to make plans for the forthcoming world conference on Faith and Order. The principal theological issue was "The Meaning of the Church and What We Mean by Unity", or in other words "The Church and the Nature of the Reunited Church". Immediately these ecumenical fathers (no women were visible!) saw that their new "spirit of conference" would eventually have to lead to a consideration of specific sorts of unity. They were clear in rejecting any model which countenanced coercion, uniformity, proselytism, expectation of a "return" to the so-called mother church, mild federation or mutual toleration, or a "spiritual" unity which did not require some visible expression. All these fall short of what is meant in the New Testament by the unity of the church, they declared.

When the first world conference on Faith and Order did gather at Lausanne in 1927, the agenda dealt with an ambitious group of issues — motivation towards unity, the nature and proclamation of the gospel, the nature of the church, the common confession of faith, ministry, sacraments, and the intriguing topic of "The Unity of Christendom and the Relation Thereto of Existing Churches". This latter issue, which is at the heart of the theme of this paper, met with extreme difficulties. The critical section of the Lausanne report (Section VII) dealt with "the idea of one church united in the essentials of faith and order, and including diverse types of doctrinal statement and the administration of church ordinances". The essential ingredients of a united church, they proposed, are:
1) a common faith, a common message to the world;
2) baptism as the rite of incorporation into the one church;
3) holy communion as expressing the corporate life of the church and its signal act of corporate worship;
4) the ministry accepted throughout the universal church;
5) freedom of interpretation about sacramental grace and ministerial order and authority;
6) due provision for the exercise of the prophetic gift. [12]

On the floor of the Lausanne conference heavy debate centred on this report. The Orthodox and certain Anglicans resisted its approval because any guarantee of "freedom of interpretation" related to sacramental grace and ministerial orders would compromise the ancient Tradition. When revised drafts could not win approval, the delegates referred the report to the Continuation Committee for later consideration and editing. At Lausanne the matter of models of union was front and centre, but the movement's maturity had not reached the point where any agreed design was possible.

The second world conference on Faith and Order at Edinburgh in 1938 also gave extensive consideration to the models of church unity. A special preparatory commission on the church's unity in life and worship presented its report on *The Meanings of Unity*, [13] with a particular section on "the forms of likeness basic for church unity". Three models or "forms of unity" were accepted by the Edinburgh conference: cooperative action (confederation for the purpose of common witness "without violation of conscience"), mutual recognition and intercommunion (the interchange of members and ministers as well as regular and mutual sacramental sharing), and corporate or organic union ("the unity of a living organism, with the diversity characteristic of the members of a healthy body... a church so united the ultimate loyalty of every member would be given to the whole body and not to any part of it"). The third model, organic union, was considered the most significant expression of the church's God-given unity; the other two models were considered partial realizations of the ultimate goal. The model or models which will bring about true unity will achieve a unity in which diversity is expressed within full communion. "Our task", concluded the Edinburgh conference, "is to find in God, to receive from God as His gift, a unity which can take up and preserve in one beloved community all the varied spiritual gifts which He has given us in our separations."[14]

RECENT DIALOGUE ON MODELS OF UNITY

The New Delhi and Nairobi conceptions of unity pressed the churches into fuller discussion of the particular forms or models of unity. This discussion, which began in the mid-1970s, has been both polemical and collegial. Ecumenical history reveals the churches' reflections were enlivened by several factors. (1) The measure of consensus which was achieved so far about the vision of unity gave an easier point of reference when evaluating the various models. (2) The Western churches' crisis of identity and the resurgence of denominational or confessional identities created a hesitancy about what the ecumenical movement had said before. A growing distrust of all institutions gave a negative flavour to any proposals for structures of unity. (3) Also the sensitivity to the divisions which now tear the human family apart — poverty, racism, economic injustice, et al. — has led to a refocusing of the ecumenical problematic. The result has been an animated dialogue, even debate, which is helping to clarify for a new generation of theologians, church leaders, pastors, and lay people, the nature of the unity we are seeking. Critical reflection on these current models is an essential part of the agenda for the teaching of ecumenics. Among the many models which have found favour in different arenas, five shall be explored in this paper.

Organic or corporate union

Organic union is the long-favoured model of the Faith and Order movement and still remains a viable option for many. In recent years, however, it is being questioned — as are all the models we shall consider — and has become something of an endangered species among some confessional and liberation theologians and some Christian World Communions. This attitude is due largely to unfortunate caricatures which have been placed upon this form of unity. Organic union has also suffered primarily from those critics who project upon it a static, monochrome image. Organic union is not a call primarily for organizational merger, or colourless theological compromises, or the consuming of the varied traditions by some monolithic mentality. Those who are open to dialogue are aware that organic union is a dynamic model, one which — in responding to the changing cultural situation and to the experience of the recent decades — has changed somewhat the texture of what is meant by this model of visible unity.

What precisely is the essence of organic union? In general it describes both an act and a state of being, much like marriage, by which previously separated church entities come together in faith, worship and sacramental life, ministry and mission —

all the ingredients of a fully shared life as identified by the New Delhi-Nairobi vision. The necessary conditions of organic union, as normally conceived, and laid out in 1970 by the conference of united and uniting churches at Limuru, Kenya, include:

> A common basis of faith; a common name; full commitment to one another, including the readiness to give up separate identity; the possibility of taking decisions together and of carrying out the missionary task as circumstances require. [15]

We can in addition list other characteristics which identify the nature of unity as offered through organic union. (1) It is a model which seeks to bring all aspects of the church's life and mission into "one fully committed fellowship". (2) Organic union is committed to the discovery of a form which represents unity-in-diversity, and to achieving a fellowship in which authentic diversity is honoured and encouraged and in which authentic unity and communion are experienced. (3) While it in no sense proposes a political or business merger or the merger of all church organizations, organic union does assume the importance of common structure and order. This implies local and universal structures of common accountability and enrichment in teaching the faith and in fulfilling Christ's mission in the world. The unity of the people of God, especially as it would exist between churches within the same territory, could scarcely be realized without some expression in structures of ecclesial relationship and service. (4) Organic union is a costly act in that churches are asked to offer their confessional or denominational identities to the larger wholeness of the body. In the language of the New Delhi statement, which affirmed organic union as the goal: "The achievement of unity will involve nothing less than a death or rebirth of many forms of church life as we have known them. We believe that nothing less costly can finally suffice." In this commitment organic union in no way denies the spiritual gifts that have come through these traditions; only a denial of their divisive nature is sought, while seeking to mingle them in a wider experience of catholicity. (5) Finally, the shape of the church's unity attained through organic union is designed to be a visible sign of the unity of humankind in a particular place. Such a united church would creatively embody the distinctive religious experiences of minority groups and those Christians who have been marginalized by the traditional ecclesiological configurations.

Conciliar fellowship

As we have seen, "conciliar fellowship" as a model of unity emerged as an elaboration of organic unity. It contains the essential elements recognized by most churches today as indispensable for visible church unity — the mutual recognition of the fullness of the catholicity of other churches, common witness to the same apostolic faith, mutual sharing of baptism and the eucharist, recognition of each other's members and ministries, joint mission and service in the world.

At the centre of this model is the commitment to understand unity as a unity of "local churches" which are "truly united". One of the characteristics of this model is its trans-confessional nature, i.e. it proposes a union of the previously divided congregations and local churches and a reconciling of rich diversity of the previously divided denominations or confessions. Such a possibility often raises fears and concerns among those who believe confessional identities are the most vital expression of the church. In a united church of conciliar fellowship, however, the confessions or traditions would not be denied or abandoned. Nor would their particular witness to universality be swept away. Such a visible unity would, however, reconcile the divisions which these confessions represent and which obscure their witness to Christ's mission to all humankind. Furthermore the model of conciliar fellowship calls for representative conciliar gatherings, structures of common decision-making, which would be manifestations of visible unity. This has been described as "a genuinely universal council", much like the ancient ecumenical councils, through which the church in our time can make common decisions about its faith and mission. Conciliarity in this sense touches deeply the ways and various levels in which the churches relate to each other and respond together to their mission and their environment. Finally, the vision of the one church as a conciliar fellowship is an expression of the inclusive participation of the people of God from their many cultures, races, and nationalities. It assumes that the participation of all Christians, especially those who have been marginalized by racism, poverty, or other forms of exclusion, is an expression of catholicity.

Reconciled diversity

This model of unity was developed in the mid-1970s amid the renascence of the World Confessional Families or, as they are now known, Christian World Commmunions. The Faith and Order Commission invited these bodies to reflect on their ecclesial identity and "to clarify their understanding of the quest for unity". The resultant model of "reconciled diversity" emerged from the insights and experiences of the international bilateral dialogues and became one of the positions in the ecumenical discussion. The theological work on "reconciled diversity" has so far been primarily at the initiative of Lutheran theologians in Europe and the Lutheran World Federation (e.g. the Dar-es-Salaam Assembly, 1977).

This model, like conciliar fellowship and organic union, assumes the constitutive elements of full church unity are agreement on the one apostolic faith, fellowship in baptism and the eucharist, and mutual recognition of ordained ministries. What is distinctive is its understanding of what constitutes church division and what is the ecumenical role of denominational or confessional identities and heritages. Advocates of reconciled diversity accept confessional identity, e.g. Lutheran, Reformed, Roman Catholic, Anglican, Disciples, Methodist, Baptist, *et al.*, as the primary legitimate forms and expressions of the diversity of the church of Christ. These confessions express diverse spiritual gifts, and are the essential components of the universal church. A discussion paper at the 1974 conference of secretaries of Christian World Communions, entitled "The Role of the World Confessional Families in the One Ecumenical Movement", stated: "We consider the variety of denominational heritages as legitimate insofar as the truth of the one faith explicates itself in history in a variety of expressions."[16] At Dar-es-Salaam the Lutheran World Federation spoke: reconciled diversity "is a way of living encounter, spiritual experience together, theological dialogue, and mutual correction, a way in which the distinctiveness of each partner is not lost sight of but is transformed and renewed, and in this way becomes visible and palpable to the other partners as a legitimate form of Christian existence and of the one Christian faith."[17]

Accordingly, unity in no sense "entails the surrender of confessional traditions and confessional identities". These forms of the Christian faith have an abiding value in all their variety. As Harding Meyer claims: "Church unity in a full, unimpaired, and enriched form [can be achieved] even where these confessional traditions, identities and peculiarities are retained."[18] In evaluating this model other theologians offer a key caveat, namely the assumption that "the existing differences between churches will lose their divisive character" by being "transformed", "changed" and "renewed" in the process of bilateral dialogue. In its boldest form, reconciled diversity assumes that the separate confessional churches could, indeed should, continue to exist side by side at local, national, and international levels; they can be "reconciled" but remain institutionally separate.

As with all the models under discussion, reconciled diversity has a host of defenders and critics. Lutheran theologian Ulrich Duchrow believes it could "lead the churches which employ it into perilous theological error", mainly because rather than expressing faithfully the biblical concept of reconciliation it assumes the only witness to truth is the post-Reformation patterns of ecclesiological identity.[19] This raises the question as to whether denominations or confessions are the only ultimate ecclesial expression of the diversity which the gospel gives to the church. Other theologians would critique reconciled diversity for an insensitivity to the divisions of the human community and its limitation in expressing solidarity and service in a world of diverse cultures, ethnic identities, and races.

In the early days when it was first proposed, reconciled diversity was so interpreted as to be perceived as an alternative to organic union and conciliar fellowship. This bias produced a polemical situation, which proved unhelpful to the creative search for models which express the commonly agreed upon goal. Some lessening of this tension was achieved at the first forum on bilateral conversations (1978), which brought together representatives of the international bilaterals between Christian World Communions and of the multilateral conversations promoted by the Commission on Faith and Order of the World Council of Churches. This forum's report set forth two methodological agreements which are important for our continuing discussion. First, the bilaterals and the multilaterals are understood to be "complementary to one another within the one ecumenical movement", while confessing that "the closer fellowship or unity of two churches, or even of two world confessional families, still falls short of being the visible unity of all Christian people". Second, the forum made clear that organic unity (conciliar fellowship) and reconciled diversity, while different in their focus, should each be considered legitimate, provisional forms of visible church unity.[20] Undoubtedly the dialogue between these particular models constitutes an important part of the future ecumenical agenda.

Communion of communions

In some ways this model is a slight variation of "reconciled diversity", but in other ways it may speak more forcefully about the depth of unity in Christ sought by organic union and conciliar fellowship. Its significance can also be attributed to the fact that it comes from the theological reflections of the Roman Catholic Church. On the eve of Vatican II, Fr Bernard Lambert proposed that future ecumenical ecclesiology concentrate on the "typologies of the form of union", which represent the different Christian traditions through which the one gospel of Jesus Christ has been received. Emmanuel Lanne, OSB, a long-time Faith and Order participant, expanded this model by describing the image of unity as "a variety of typologies within the same ecclesial allegiance". In a revealing sentence he declared: "It is clear that we must try to discover together in what manner and measure God intends the unity of his Church to express also diversity and pluralism in a single communion of faith and church life."[21] Building on these ideas, this model was publicly and officially put on the ecumenical agenda by Cardinal Willebrands in an address at Cambridge in 1970. He proposed that the church's visible unity might be expressed in varied "types" *(typoi)* living in communion. This unity is a "plurality of types" — Roman Catholic, Baptist, Orthodox, Reformed, Anglican, *et al.* — within the communion of the one and only church of Christ. Each *typos* is distinguished by the following elements: a "characteristic theological method and perspective", a "characteristic canonical discipline", a "tradition of spirituality and devotion", a "characteristic liturgical expression". The signs of their communion would be common teaching in faith and morals, eucharist sharing, and agreements on ministry and papacy.

This model is intriguing because of its sense of balance. It reveals a sensitivity to the diversity of traditions and spiritualities. Yet it equally places *communion*, a deep relationship, at the centre. A communion of communions would certainly not be possible unless each tradition *(typos)* undergoes significant change and renewal and each becomes an integral part of the whole fellowship. Sister churches would move beyond their separate identities into a common identity.

Unity as solidarity

A new model of unity has lately come to the ecumenical scene primarily from the experience of theologians and churches in Latin America. One who has most dynamically articulated its implications is Jon Sobrino, the Jesuit professor of theology in El Salvador.[22] For Sobrino unity and catholicity mean "co-responsibility between local churches", mutual giving and receiving, bearing one another's burdens. This costly giving and receiving extends to diverse areas in the life of the church: liturgy, pastoral relations, and the practice of faith. Such a dynamic relationship is never expressed only in a formal or abstract sense, but is always practised in concrete ways and in specific situations. Such practice is expressed fullest in "responding to God's will regarding the life and death of human beings" as well as in expressing solidarity between churches — both of which embody the essence of the church and which carry out the church's mission.

The crux of this model is not the relationship between the different confessions, but rather their common solidarity, suffering with the poor. The fundamental division in humankind, according to this model, is the alienation between the rich and the poor, between the oppressed and oppressors. The deepest divisive boundary line among Christians is, therefore, not between different confessional families. The scandal of the divided church is no longer in the division between churches or types of traditions, but between "different ways of living the faith in a Christian and ecclesial manner, and this division runs through the diverse confessions".[23] The essence of this division is not the contrast between formulations of the faith or orders of ministry. The scandalous division is between those who live and those who die; the deepest reality of brokenness is those situations where the unity of the human race which God promised and gives to all persons in Jesus Christ is denied.

What this model implies for the traditional pursuit of models of unity is rather traumatic. It says that unless models of unity are committed to solidarity with the poor and oppressed, they will create a unity which is, at best, marginal in expressing the fellowship of believers. Only as the churches together face "the fundamental division" and overcome "the primary scandal" will they discover their legitimate unity — a unity in solidarity and suffering. Interconfessional unity without prior solidarity with the poor of this world "is out of touch with reality, anti-Christian, and difficult to achieve in real history".

Bishop Lesslie Newbigin makes a similar case in his 1983 Peter Ainslie Lecture on Christian Unity. "Unity in Christ", he says, "is a kind of mutual solidarity which requires all the members to take the same kind of responsibility for one another as is implied in Paul's metaphor of the body."[24] The united church is "the company of those who follow the Lamb". Such a form of visible unity offers guidance for, and indeed judgment on, all models of unity, and poses two principles which come from the ministry of Jesus Christ. First, says Newbigin, any relevant model will express "the principle of leadership in the way of the cross". Just as to follow Jesus is to go the way of the cross, so participation in the cross is an essential aspect in the discovery of the church's unity. To translate this insight into an ecclesiology is a demanding exercise. It requires churches to choose a model of unity which will minimize self-aggrandize-ment or preoccupation with internal matters. It calls for leadership — among bishops, presbyters, deacons, and lay people — which will make decisions that are costly in personal gain by opposing the scandalous division of poverty, racism, sexism, and war.

The second principle for a relevant form of unity includes "the supreme care for the marginal". Again the teaching and practice of Jesus furnish our clues. He cared without limits for the outcasts, the poor, the untouchables, those whom others rejected. Unity which is modelled on Jesus' ministry will be inclusive of "the least of these". No confession of faith, no eucharistic fellowship, no ministry or strategies for common mission which do not embrace the faithful, full participation of those who have lived on the periphery of power and privilege will bring authentic unity. When our unity conversations include, in this sense, the marginalized among the people of God, the church will discover its wholeness and be able to function as a sign, instrument and foretaste of God's intention of reconciliation for a desperately divided human race. "The struggle for Christian unity", says Newbigin, "cannot be severed from the recovery of a genuinely missionary confrontation with our so-called modern culture in which the church will be seen again as the *ecclesia tou Theou*, the Assembly to which God summons *all* peoples and in which no other sovereignty is recognized but this."[25]

Conclusion

These reflections on the major models of unity and union have taken us to the heart of the ecumenical task. We have seen the quest for visible unity — God's gift and our task — as an encounter with the integrity of the church. None of the models we have considered is *the* model. Nor can any one of them claim infallibility or universal acceptance. Likewise power plays for one or the other will certainly not lead the churches into truth. The discussion comes at a more humble moment. In the days ahead we need far more creative dialogue about the shape of the church and dedicated pursuit of the unity God wills for the church. We need far wider participation by ministers and lay people in the process, especially the participation of students and professors in the theological seminaries where ecumenism has been woefully eclipsed.

We need far greater understanding of models of church unity in the global context of the struggle for unity and renewal in the human community. With these perspectives the search for visible unity will become less of a political debate and more of a faith pilgrimage.

NOTES

[1] *Spaceship Earth*, New York, Columbia University Press, 1966, p. 16.
[2] W. A. Visser 't Hooft, "Pluralism — Temptation or Opportunity", *The Ecumenical Review*, Vol. XVIII, No. 2, April, 1966, p. 129.
[3] See Stanley J. Samartha, *Courage for Dialogue: Ecumenical Issues in Inter-religious Relationships*, Geneva, WCC, 1981, pp. 129 ff.
[4] *Diversity and Communion*, Mystic, Connecticut, Twenty-Third Publications, 1985, pp. 40-43.
[5] Visser 't Hooft, *op. cit.*, p. 149.
[6] *Op. cit.*, p. 16.
[7] *Global Solidarity in Theological Education: Report of US/Canadian Consultation, Toronto, Ontario, July 12-15, 1981*, Geneva, WCC Programme on Theological Education, p. 16.
[8] W. A. Visser 't Hooft, *The New Delhi Report: the Third World Assembly of the World Council of Churches, 1961*, New York, Association Press, 1962, p. 116.
[9] Norman Goodall ed., *The Uppsala Report, 1968*, Geneva, WCC, 1968, p. 13.
[10] *Ibid.*, p. 17.
[11] David M. Paton, ed., *Breaking Barriers: Nairobi 1975*, Grand Rapids, Wm. R. Eerdmans, London, SPCK, 1976, p. 60.
[12] H. N. Bate ed., *Faith and Order: Proceedings of the World Conference on Faith and Order, August 3-21, 1927*, New York, George H. Doran Co., 1927, pp. 398 (first draft), 436 (second draft).
[13] *Faith and Order Paper No. 82*, first series.
[14] Leonard Hodgson ed., *The Second World Conference on Faith and Order Held at Edinburgh, August 3-18, 1937*, New York, The Macmillan Co., 1938, pp. 250-269.
[15] "Notes from the Limuru (1970) Conference", *Mid-Stream: an Ecumenical Journal*, Vol. IX, No. 2-3, winter-spring 1971, pp. 13-33.
[16] *WCC Exchange*, No. 3/2, July 1977.
[17] Arne Sovik ed., *In Christ — a New Community: the Proceedings of the Sixth Assembly of the Lutheran World Federation, Dar-es-Salaam, Tanzania*, June 13-25, 1977, Geneva, LWF, 1977.
[18] Gunther Gassmann and Harding Meyer, *The Unity of the Church: Requirements and Structure*, LWF report No. 15, Geneva, Lutheran World Federation, 1983, p. 9.
[19] *Conflict over the Ecumenical Movement: Confessing Christ Today in the Universal Church*, Geneva, WCC, 1981, p. 183. The revered Dominican ecumenist Yves Congar, O. P. made a similar critique in his *Diversity and Communion*, Mystic, Connecticut, Twenty-Third Publications, 1985, p. 151.
[20] "The Three Reports of the Forum on Bilateral Conversations", *Faith and Order Paper 107*, Geneva, WCC, 1981, pp. 4, 5.
[21] "Pluralism and Unity: the Possibility of a Variety of Typologies Within the Same Ecclesial Allegiance", *One in Christ*, Vol. VI, No. 3, 1970, pp. 430-451.
[22] See Jon Sobrino and Juan Hernandes Pico, *Theology of Christian Solidarity*, Maryknoll, NY, Orbis Books, 1985.
[23] *Ibid.*, p. 28.
[24] "The Basis and the Forms of Unity", *Mid-Stream: an Ecumenical Journal*, Vol. XXIII, No. 1, January 1984, pp. 1-12. (2nd Peter Ainslie Lecture on Christian Unity, 1983, an international lectureship which is sponsored each year by the Council on Christian Unity of the Disciples of Christ).
[25] *Ibid.*, p. 12.

3. An Ecumenical Approach to Teaching the Bible

John Mbiti

Introducing and supplying the Bible to our world

In a recent survey conducted in Belgium, it was reported that "60-80 percent of the six million Flemings had never seen a Bible". [1] Until 1981, the Europe Regional Centre of the United Bible Societies was in Brussels, housed in the same building with the Belgian Bible Society. Belgium is 90 percent Christian, the vast majority belonging to the Roman Catholic Church. The church there is declining.

A scripture distribution promoter in Tanzania recently drove some 700 kms to deliver Kiswahili New Testaments in Mwanza on the shores of Lake Victoria. On arrival there, "word quickly spread that the Bible man, Mboya, was in town. He was overwhelmed by crowds of people. Not only did he suffer physically, but eager customers attacked the vehicle in an effort to ensure a copy of this much-prized New Testament for themselves. One door was almost ripped from its hinges, and paintwork and car body were damaged. Another day the need will be met, but meanwhile eager hands wait." [2] Some 55 percent of Tanzania's population today is Christian, representing many church traditions. The church is growing there as it is in the southern two-thirds of Africa.

These two reports among many similar accounts from all over the world illustrate two important considerations. First, the teaching of the Bible in ecumenical perspectives has to tackle the question of bringing the Bible to the Christians. In areas of older Christendom the Bible is often either an unknown book, or lies closed on book shelves. How can the Bible be brought to the people, to the Christians, so that they can see it, handle it, read it, understand parts of it and make use of its contents? In the richer countries, it is not that the people are illiterate, nor that they cannot afford to buy a copy of the Bible. Those who know the Bible, those who teach about it or otherwise use it, are challenged here to introduce the Bible to the masses in such a way that it will be seen and bought, bought and read, read and applied. Yes, so that the Bible in fact can read the people. The people have to be introduced to the Bible and the Bible introduced to them. That is a major ecumenical challenge.

Then there is the fact that there are areas of our one world where the Bible is such a precious book that people (Christians) fight to get a copy of it, or have to save money in order to buy a copy. In some cases they even obtain copies through a system of smuggling, or buying them as stolen goods. It is reported that some

Christians in China have (had) to copy out the Bible by hand, to ensure that they get a copy or part of it. Here, then, the basic problem is how to supply and how to obtain Bibles where they are desperately needed and intensively read. We cannot teach the Bible effectively to people who do not have it, especially in their own languages. Many countries have Bible Societies which carry out the enormous task of translating, supplying and distributing the scriptures. These Bible Societies are often ecumenical. Their work could be given more attention and recognition in churches and theological faculties and seminaries than is often the case, to say nothing about financial support for them.

Ignorance about the very existence of the Bible and problems connected with obtaining it are fundamental challenges to the task of teaching the scriptures.

The Bible as the book of the whole world (oikoumene)

Up to the beginning of this century, the Bible was largely a book of the northern part of the world, just as Christianity itself was centred in the north. I use the term north to mean North America, Europe and the Soviet Union. The term south refers to Africa, Asia, Latin America and Oceania. The history of the church had been largely an event of the north, even though the Christian faith, like Judaism, had begun in Asia. But the bulk of Christian scholarship, theology, spirituality, liturgy, art and even heresies, had occurred in the north. In contrast, the south had become marginalized and, through the modern missionary movement as well as the shifting of political power, it had been edged to the receiving end of nearly all things Christian. The imbalance was overwhelming. To enter into the world of Christian scholarship (and particularly biblical) one had to learn and use not just the main biblical languages of Hebrew and Greek, but also Latin, Italian, English, German, French and in some cases Russian and Spanish. Many of these languages have continued to dominate theological scholarship up to today.

A great deal of valuable learning and insights came out of the northern region of Christendom. Christianity has acquired a lot of treasures from the long presence of the church in the north. We must appreciate this rich heritage gathered through the centuries, whatever criticisms we may want to make. Through the grace of God, the north has given and can still give much to the rest of Christendom out of the long history of the church.

The Bible was destined to speak to the peoples of the whole world, not only through the main languages of the north but also through the languages of the south. Up to 1900, the Bible had been translated in full or in part into 537 languages (of which 124 were complete Bibles, with 44.4 percent being in languages of the north, and 55.6 percent in the south). The New Testament was available in 239 languages (of which 34 percent were in the north and 66 percent in the south).

In the course of this century, several factors have speeded up the number of translations of the Bible into the world's languages. By 1980, the Bible was available in 1,811 languages, of which 15 percent were in the north and 85 percent in the south. The complete Bible was available in 276 languages, 22.8 percent in the north and 77.2 percent in the south. The New Testament was available in 759 languages, of which 13.6 percent were in the north and 86.4 percent in the south.

These statistics lead us to draw several important consequences of what has happened and what should happen.

a) While the Bible has come down in history as largely a book of the north, it has now become geographically and statistically a book of southern languages and overwhelmingly so when we compare 15 percent northern languages with 85 percent southern languages.

b) The fundamental reality is that the Bible has now become the book of the whole world, of the oikoumene. The peoples of the whole world can read it, hear it read, integrate it into their Christian thought-system and life (or raise questions about it) in their own languages. This they can do, in the spirit of Pentecost: "We hear them telling in our own tongues the mighty works of God" (Acts 2:11).

c) The availability of the Bible in an ever-increasing number of languages in the south has been a contributing factor in the rapid increase of Christians in this region. Here in particular we include the southern two-thirds of Africa, South Korea and the Pacific region where Christianity is spreading most rapidly today.[3] Up to 1980, the majority of Christians lived in the north. For example, in 1900, 82.8 percent of all Christians were in the north, and only 17.2 percent lived in the south. In 1970, 57.3 percent were in the north and 42.7 percent in the south. In 1980, 51.2 percent were in the north and 48.8 percent in the south. By 1985 the north had 48.5 percent and the south 51.5 percent. It is forecast that if this trend continues, in the year 2000 AD the Christians in the north will account for 39.7 percent and in the south 60.3 percent of the total Christendom.

d) While the north has been the historical centre of the Bible, today the south has become the statistical and geographical centre of the Bible. Putting the two together, we come up with the conclusion that the Bible has become a truly ecumenical book, a book of the oikoumene. It is the most shared book in the history and geography of the world. Nobody can monopolize it. No language can monopolize its secrets and difficulties. No church tradition can monopolize the interpretation of its contents. No school of theology can monopolize the theological application of the Bible. The Bible bounces beyond all boundaries; it speaks some two thousand languages (used by about 90 percent of the world's inhabitants).

e) The Bible has now become so thoroughly ecumenical that it cannot be taught meaningfully, nor understood meaningfully, without this ecumenical perspective. We enter into the Bible as individuals, as schools of thought, church traditions or native speakers of particular languages. But when the Bible enters into us, it comes as an ecumenical and multilingual book. Ecumenical teaching of the Old and the New Testament means not only that we learn to read them, but rather that they read us,[4] they enter into our world as ecumenical scriptures. We cannot afford to read and teach the Bible as though it were exclusively a German or English or Korean or Kiswahili Bible. That would not be ecumenical but provincial; it would be not only a dull exercise, but one that leads ultimately to ecumenical malnutrition and starvation. How can we approach the Bible and teach it in a given context or situation but as a book of the whole world? Teaching the Bible is or should be the opposite of playing in the football world cup competition in which the different teams go on knocking each other out until finally one team wins the golden cup. Teaching and reading the Bible in ecumenical perspectives means that each team starts with the golden cup itself and gives others to drink the water of life out of the golden cup. It is an act of communion (koinonia) and not one of competition, an act of incorporating others and not one of silencing them.

Biblical symbols in ecumenical perspectives

The Bible is full of symbols, which had their immediate meanings when originally applied. Biblical and textual criticism helps throw light upon their original or continued usage. The symbols have not remained static, nor can they. The ecumenization of the Bible demands also the ecumenization of biblical symbols and our understanding of them.

The two most fundamental symbols are God in the Old Testament and Jesus Christ in the New Testament, if for the sake of discussion we may call these "symbols". God is also very present in the New Testament, being revealed most concretely by and through Jesus Christ. God is introduced in the Bible as "ecumenical" God: "In the beginning God created the heavens and the earth" (Gen. 1:1). This is repeated in the New Testament: "In the beginning was the word... He was in the beginning with God; all things were made through him, and without him was not anything made that was made" (John 1:1-3). These are the settings for the symbols of God and of Jesus Christ, and the Bible should be seen as the unfolding of the ecumenical perspectives of the two symbols.

We recognize, however, that at times and in places God in the Old Testament is presented as though God were exclusively of one people, Israel. In the New Testament, God and Jesus Christ are sometimes seen or presented as if they were exclusively Christian property. In many passages of the Bible reference is made to the God "of Israel", "of Abraham, Jacob and Isaac". But I do not see these passages as putting a monopoly on God. Rather, they are passages to emphasize the "covenant" relationship between God and humankind, with Israel as a representative of the oikoumene. Indeed, God's calling of Abraham (Abram) is for the sole purpose of executing the ecumenical outreach in the world: "Go from your country and your kindred and your father's house... I will bless you, and make your name great, so that you will be a blessing... in you *all the families* of the earth shall be blessed" (Gen. 12:1-3).

There is a common beginning, an ecumenical beginning to creation, to humanity (in Adam and Eve). There is also an ecumenical promise (covenant with Noah, with Abraham and on Sinai) which runs through the Old Testament. When we come to the New Testament, there is an ecumenical centre in Jesus Christ. He becomes the fulfilment of God's promise and at the same time the new promise for the completion of all things. So St Paul could write, with the Old Testament very much in his heart and mind: "When the time had fully come, God sent forth his Son, born of a woman" (Gal. 4:4): "For he has made known to us in all wisdom and insight the mystery of his will, according to his purpose which he set forth in Christ as a plan for the fullness of time, to unite all things in him, things in heaven and things on earth" (Eph. 1:9, 10).

There is clearly an ecumenical origin of things, there is an ecumenical promise (or series of promises, covenants), there is an ecumenical centre in Jesus Christ and there is an ecumenical eschatological goal to which all things are moving. I imagine that teaching the Bible in ecumenical perspectives demands putting the biblical symbols under this ecumenical umbrella. The list of these symbols is without limit. The main ones include, besides God and Jesus Christ, People of God, Slavery and Liberation, Covenant, the Human Person, Promise and Fulfilment, Spirit and Holy Spirit, Church as the Body of Christ, Salvation, Kingdom of God, Sin, Death and Resurrection, Faith and Hope, Eschatology, and so on. If we approach these symbols under the ecumenical umbrella, then they will acquire very broad perspectives.

The need to reconsider biblical symbols is also being pressed upon us by some of the technological and scientific developments of our time. For example the whole advance of knowledge on the potential of nuclear power challenges us to re-examine traditional concepts on history and eschatology. Since Hiroshima on Transfiguration Day in 1945, the human being has become not only co-worker with God but a potential destroyer of life on the earth. The nuclear accident in Chernobyl in April 1986 is a reminder that the human being can destroy the earth, in full or in part, without deliberately pressing the button. Hiroshima, Chernobyl and others have ecumenical consequences for our study of the scriptures and biblical symbols. Cain was asked by the Lord: "Where is Abel your brother?" He said: " I do not know; am I my brother's keeper?" (Gen. 4:9). Jesus was asked: "And who is my neighbour?" (Luke 10:29). When or if the Bible reads us in the light of these questions, it would give us directions to search for answers which the nuclear age demands of the users of the scriptures.[5] Are we not already being forced to make our biblical studies wearing anti-radiation masks? After Hiroshima, Psalm 8 takes on a frightfully new meaning: "What is man that thou art mindful of him, and the son of man that thou dost care for him? Yet thou hast made him little less than God, and dost crown him with glory and honour. Thou hast given him dominion over the works of thy hands..." (8:4-6).

Opportunities for teaching the Bible in ecumenical perspective

There are increasingly many opportunities for teaching or using the scriptures with specific ecumenical orientations. Indeed, the potential for ecumenical orientation in biblical studies has always been there, but it has not always been exploited. Instead, denominational, cultural and doctrinal provincialism has tended to choke or retard the ecumenical orientation. The translation and availability of the Bible (in full or in part) in some 2000 languages of the world is a challenge to some of this provincialism. At the same time, these translations plus the fact that Christendom is slowly shifting to the southern summer, offer us new opportunities for ecumenical reading, teaching and using of the Bible. Some of these opportunities have more weight in certain situations or regions than in others. We mention a few here, without going into details.

Inter-religious dialogue

The southern region of the world to which Christianity has begun to shift statistically has many other religions like Islam, Hinduism, Buddhism, tribal religions and so on. These religions have been part and parcel of the history, culture, world-view, spirituality, ethics and the general orientation of life. Not only has the Bible now to be read within the contexts of these religions, but it is one among many other sacred scriptures (some of which are not even written down but are transmitted orally).

In this area, there are two considerations in teaching the Bible. It should be approached as one among many sacred writings of the world. Such an approach says nothing about the authority and interpretation of the Bible as such, nor about the question of inspiration. These issues have occupied the church almost throughout its history. In various meetings of the Faith and Order Commission of the World Council of Churches they have received a lot of attention and we have no need to take them up here in this paper.[6] But the Bible addresses itself to human themes about which other religions (and their scriptures) have also something to say. The Bible has no monopoly on religious concerns and problems.

Secondly, the Bible has something to say on the major issues of dialogue. We should so approach it that we find in it theological insights for engaging in dialogue. It should speak not only to the Jews (the Old Testament) and Christians (Old and New Testaments), but to people of other faiths.[7] Some of the major areas of inter-religious dialogue include: creation, scriptures, Christology, salvation, mission and witness, spirituality, community, hope and vision.[8] What passages of the Bible speak to these topics? How can we understand these passages side by side with passages from the scriptures of other religions? What do people of other faiths say to these biblical passages? What light does the Bible throw on the passages of other scriptures that deal with these themes?

Peace and justice

These are major ecumenical concerns of our day. Indeed they transcend Christian circles. Politicians talk day and night about them, whatever their deeds may say. Since the Bible has become an ecumenical book, what it says about these concerns should be brought out to question, support, undermine or simply illuminate theologically the discussions and activities relating to these concerns. The relevant passages of the Bible lend themselves to ecumenical usage, even if political ideologies and dreams may sometimes cause rifts in the use of those passages. For example, in the present climate of arms reduction discussions between the United States and the Soviet Union, how would we teach ecumenically the famous passage from Isaiah 2:4, which says: "He (God) shall judge between the nations, and shall decide for many peoples; and they shall beat their swords into plowshares, and their spears into pruning hooks; nation shall not lift up sword against nation, neither shall they learn war any more"? Which other passages of the Old Testament and of the New Testament come alive in the struggle for peace and justice? Does an ecumenical approach to them enhance or weaken their relevance and potentiality in wrestling with these issues? Since many other religions also concern themselves with these issues, how do we accommodate their voices in our one ecumenical world?

The Bible in ecumenical services and activities

Increasingly Christians the world over come together for church worship and other joint activities. These are golden opportunities for teaching and using the Bible in ecumenical perspectives. The celebration of key feasts or periods of the church year, the observance of the Week of Prayer for Christian Unity, the Women's World Day of Prayer, the Observance of the Week of Peace (in autumn or during Lent, for example, in West Germany), local and international conferences, these and many others lend themselves to biblical teaching. There are countries, for example, Kenya, Tanzania and Uganda, where the teaching of religious education (heavily oriented to Bible knowledge) is done on the basis of an ecumenical syllabus drawn up by Anglican, Roman Catholic and Protestant churches. The teaching of the Bible in African universities is carried out on an academic basis without regard to denominational orientation. This is the case in universities in some other countries in the world, where the trend is more for departments of religious studies rather than departments (or faculties) of theology (whether Roman Catholic or Reformed or Protestant). Where these opportunities are utilized, the Bible opens itself more and more for an ecumenical approach, which in turn unlocks more of its riches for the people of God. Rightly the Evangelische Kirche in Deutschland (EKD) recently said in a publication to encourage ecumenical encounters: "Ecumenical learning means, therefore, through others and with one another, learning to understand the Bible deeper. At the same time it means, to discover in biblical statements the problems and perspectives which are essential for the understanding of ecumenism. Ecumenical learning leads to the Bible and grows out of the Bible."[9]

The Lima document on "Baptism, Eucharist and Ministry"
The BEM document has given churches throughout the world, since Vancouver 1983, a great opportunity to study and discuss it in the light of the Bible. Even long after the deadline for collecting official responses from the churches is over, this document will continue to be studied (in whatever modified form after the responses).

Nature and ecology
These are current issues of concern the world over. They embrace questions of survival not only for human beings but for nature at large. Nature poses questions that transcend national, cultural and ecclesiastical boundaries. They are ecumenical questions of great magnitude. What does the Bible teach us about nature? What do other religions contribute towards our understanding of the relationship between God, humankind and nature? How do we approach passages like the ecological doxology of Psalm 104? Our knowledge of nature, as well as the various ways in which individuals and society inflict wounds upon nature today through various forms of pollution, exploitation, interruption of ecological balance and even contamination with radiation, has increased tremendously in the last two centuries. To what extent can we share or dispute the hope of T. F. Torrance that "man, humbled and awed by the mysterious intelligibility of the universe that reaches far beyond his powers, will learn to fulfil his destined role as the servant of divine love and the priest of creation"?[10]

We are challenged to reflect theologically and biblically on nature and ecology. Does nature, for example, also have rights which must be respected, protected and even restored to it? Is nature one big parable of God, out of which Jesus took some pieces to teach about the kingdom of God?

Bible and culture
The more languages into which the Bible is translated, the more cultures it enters. Ecumenical encounter is also encounter across cultures. The invasion of all parts of the world by the politically and technologically more powerful cultures of the West has evoked fears of cultural imperialism, the loss of cultural identity and the stigmatization of many of the other cultures as "primitive, heathen and uncivilized". There is plenty of room for the Bible to throw light on the question of culture when the Christian faith is introduced into a given culture, as well as upon cultures which have had the gospel for many generations. For example, missionaries have condemned the custom of polygamous families in African and other societies where Western missionaries introduced the gospel. These same missionaries, together with their African (or other) converts, translate the Bible into local languages. Christians read it in the framework of their culture and discover, among other things, that great pillars of the faith in the Old Testament were actually polygamous — such as Abraham, Jacob, Moses and David. The Bible, they see, neither encourages nor condemns polygamy — at least,

seen through cultures other than Western. Single cultures may tend to blind our understanding of some parts of the Bible; ecumenical openness is certainly an enrichment in our understanding the Bible and in applying its insights. The church continues to be faced with the question of relating the gospel to culture, be that tribal settings or within the world-class cities.

Concluding remarks

I do not have a model for teaching the Bible in ecumenical perspectives. A few principles and questions could be thrown on the table for further discussion.

1. The Bible is still a living book. It should be taught and studied as such. Examples of this can be seen in the minjung theology in Korea, in the struggle for liberation in South Africa, and in the way the church survived in China since 1949. If the Bible is not taught as a living book, people lose interest in it. How do we make it a living book?

2. The Bible comes first to people; afterwards they come to it. It has travelled a long distance in time and space. It will continue to travel. It has become a book of and for the whole world (oikoumene). How can we increase our ecumenical pilgrimage to it and with it?

3. The Bible is a uniting factor, at least potentially. How can peoples of many cultures and church traditions be drawn to this uniting process in the one Bible?

4. The Bible in the one world is the sacred book of one religious tradition (Judeo-Christian) out of many other religions. What limits as well as potentials does this fact put upon the Bible? What responsibilities are entailed in teaching it?

NOTES

[1] EPD (Schweiz. Evangel. Pressedienst), Nr 16, 24 April 1986, Zürich, p.1.

[2] UBS (United Bible Society), World Report 193, June 1986, p.10.

[3] See further: David B. Barrett, "The Spread of the Bible and the Growth of the Church in Africa", *Bulletin: United Bible Societies*, No. 128/129, third/fourth quarters 1982, pp.5-18; John S. Mbiti, *Bible and Theology in African Christianity*, Oxford, 1986; Cyris H. S. Moon, *A Korean Minjung Theology*, Orbis Books, 1985; *International Review of Mission*, Vol. LXXIV, No. 293, January 1985. The statistics in this paper come largely from David B. Barrett ed., *World Christian Encyclopedia*, Oxford, 1982.

[4] This is not my original idea as such, as I have come across it in a few places. See a recent discussion of it by John B. Rogers, Jr, " The Book That Reads Us", *Interpretation: a Journal of Bible and Theology*, Vol. XXXIX, No. 4, October 1985, pp.388ff.

[5] See further discussion by Gordon D. Kaufman, *Theology for a Nuclear Age*, Manchester and Philadelphia, 1985.

[6] See the account of these discussions in Ellen Flesseman-van Leer ed., *The Bible, its Authority and Interpretation in the Ecumenical Movement*, Geneva, WCC, 1980.

[7] See further discussion by Wesley Ariarajah, *The Bible and People of Other Faiths*, Geneva, WCC, 1985.

[8] This list of themes is taken from a study booklet, *Theological Discoveries Through Interfaith Dialogue*, currently under preparation for publication by the WCC, Geneva, late 1986.

[9] *Ökumenisches Lernen*, edited by the Kirchenamt der Evangelischen Kirche in Deutschland, Gütersloh, 1985.

[10] *The Ground and Grammar of Theology*, Charlottesville, Virginia, 1980, p.14. See an earlier discussion by Thomas Sieger Derr, *Ecology and Human Liberation*, Geneva, WSCF, 1973.

4. Bible Study from a Latin American Angle

Procoro Velasques

In order rightly to understand what is going on in the field of biblical interpretation (as in other theological disciplines) in Latin America, it is necessary to have some sense of the social history of the Latin American people. Latin American interpretation can only be understood by people involved in the struggle against oppression and poverty.

The Bible came to Latin America with the Protestant missionaries and the colporteurs of the Bible societies, in the middle of the last century. The Protestant missionaries had various theological approaches. The Presbyterians (who came from Princeton in the United States of America) were fundamentalist Puritans who taught that the Bible had been dictated by God and could only be read literally. For them, it teaches us the way to heaven and only those who read it can possess absolute truth and salvation. On the other hand, the Methodist and Baptist missionaries (also from the USA) were marked by the Pietistic Revival and they read the Bible "for the heart".

Despite these divergences between the missionaries, their ideological views converged in a synthesis which has become the main characteristic of Latin American Protestantism. This is a mixture of dogmatism and Puritan moralism, combined with the mystical subjectivism of Pietism and the enthusiasm of religious revival. In addition to all of this, the Protestants became terrible enemies of the Roman Catholics and of anything that had to do with Catholicism. In point of fact they had another enemy, the Liberals, who had also come as missionaries to organize theological schools and seminaries.

The colporteurs were lay people who penetrated more or less everywhere to distant villages and into the jungle to sell their portions of the Bible and distribute evangelistic pamphlets. They were more responsible than the missionaries for spreading a certain way of reading the Bible. They established small congregations (the missionaries followed them to organize these congregations and link them to their missions), Sunday schools and Bible study classes. The leaders of these groups were also lay people without any formal theological training, who went on repeating the same interpretation that they had learnt from the lay people before them. From generation to generation down to our time the reading of the Bible remained unchanged.

Protestant evangelization comprised a cultural conversion to an "Anglo-Saxon" style of life and scale of values. The missionaries who brought the gospel themselves became typical ideals to imitate. Their way of dressing, their taste in music, their thinking and their traditions, all became the model to be adopted.

The Catholic missions arrived in Latin America at the beginning of the sixteenth century in the wake of the Spanish and Portuguese colonists. Their religion was that of the crown. They were there simply to sacralize colonization with the aim of transforming the colonized into servants of the king and of the church.

In contrast to their Protestant counterparts, the Catholic missionaries arrived without the Bible, and this situation remained unchanged until our time. It was only the priests and some intellectual lay people who had the privilege of owning and reading the scriptures. This picture began to change only after Vatican II. That was the time when the Catholics began to place the Bible in the hands of the people.

Whereas the Protestant exegetes were trained in the United States of America, the Catholics studied in Europe. Thus for very many years the exegesis done in Latin America was only a reproduction (and a very bad one at that) of the exegesis in the North (USA and Europe).

The renewal of exegesis in Latin America (among both Protestants and Catholics) began at the time of the greatest oppression by the military dictatorships which had established themselves more or less everywhere in Latin America at the beginning of the 1960s. Although they were very firm from an academic point of view, the exegetical foundations from the North proved unable to provide the right instruments for dialogue and evangelization in situations of crisis. It became evident that such an exegesis was merely an instrument of social domination (political, economic and cultural) with a strong ideological background derived from the countries of the North. That exegesis had no meaning for the missionary aims of Christians involved in the process of the liberation of the oppressed and the poor in Latin America.

Thus Latin American exegesis was born in a situation of orphanhood (in relation to the exegesis of the North), in the midst of incredible social struggles against the oppression which had created and maintained poverty. It is true that the spiritualized exegesis of the conservative Protestants and that which came from the North were unable to answer the questions posed by the oppressed and the poor, because this exegesis had been done by and for the rich, namely those who had an interest in maintaining the status quo. Therefore it was necessary to find another approach.

The first step along this path was a political, revolutionary exegesis as part of an effort to respond to the crisis situation through which the continent was going, to keep the church alive and provide a different identity. But this political, revolutionary exegesis was still too similar to that being done in the Northern hemisphere (political theology and theology of revolution). However, it was half way there and a break with traditional exegesis.

The true identity of Latin American exegesis began to take shape once there was political and pastoral involvement in the communities of the poor and the oppressed. This political and pastoral activity preceded the academic work of the exegetes. They became involved in the "grassroots" movements and in the associations of those living in the poor suburbs on the periphery, in the trade unions of the workers and farmers, in the movements of blacks, women, indigenous peoples, tramps and other marginal groups. They began to discover that the majority of people had no roof over their heads, no land to farm, lived in shanty towns (*favelas*), could not read and were almost permanently unemployed. In short, there were thousands of oppressed and poor people living on the fringe of the consumer society and of the church.

39

It was necessary to re-establish contact with these people, to enter into dialogue with them and to tell them about the liberation which comes from Christ. The type of evangelization they were speaking about was no longer the salvation of the soul nor the knowledge of the truth of the revelation. It was the evangelization of the person as a whole and also of the structures of society.

The attempts to do Bible study with groups of the oppressed and the poor according to the traditional method, where the preacher or teacher talked all the time and explained the biblical text as if he/she were the only person authorized to do so, were a complete failure. This kind of method worked very well with the content of traditional exegesis but did not work at all with an exegesis that was involved in political and pastoral action for liberation. And the reason for this failure was quite clear: when a text is explained according to the traditional method, it necessarily goes through the ideological and cultural filter both of the expositor and of the listener. Therefore it was necessary to reverse the process. Firstly, it was important to learn to listen; then it was necessary to grasp the world-view (ideology and culture) of those with whom one was speaking. The third step was to identify with their struggles. The fourth was an effort to read the Bible in a new way, with the eyes of the oppressed and the poor, in order to discover God's message within it (which had deliberately been forgotten for a long time). Finally, this message had to be put in a language comprehensible to those with whom one was speaking.

It must be made quite clear that Latin American exegesis is in no way concerned about the criticisms to which it is subjected in the North, namely that it has adopted a particular ideological stand (Marxist) in opposition to the camouflaged (capitalist) ideology in traditional exegesis; and that it is in danger of becoming increasingly superficial the more it turns its back on academic exegesis.

Latin American exegesis is not yet the exegesis of the poor and the oppressed. It is still the work of intellectuals. Naturally, they are intellectuals who have opted for the poor and oppressed. This option is evident in their motives and results. Their exegesis has stopped being informative and has become participatory, open to the overall needs of the person as a whole. Their aim is action which will transform persons and social structures.

The exegesis which is born of political and pastoral activity is oral. It is only much later on that it can be written down, worked over and intellectualized. At this second stage it must remain faithful to the method used for the first stage.

The intention of Latin American exegetes is therefore not to commit themselves to anything other than the gospel. In other words, there is no commitment to Marxism. But Marxism can certainly be used as a method for analyzing the reality of society just as the exegetes of the North use structuralism, functionalism, existentialism, etc.

The Latin American exegetes also have no intention to neglect the academic contribution from exegetes in the North. What is required is that their efforts be made available to help the poor and the oppressed. Exegesis in the North lacks a clearer, more definite and more serious political and pastoral intention.

Latin American exegesis is ecumenical by nature, in its principles and its objectives. It is not a matter of the traditional ecumenism of "interfaith" dialogues, theologians and ecclesiastical authorities. This is a spontaneous ecumenism derived from the common experience of sharing in the struggles of the oppressed and the poor. It is a path which people have followed together in search of answers to their common problems in the word of God. It is not a matter of a dogmatic discussion (or even concern) nor of controlling customs.

In this ecumenism the barriers shift from dogmas and customs to ideology. Our adversaries are no longer those whose dogmas and customs are different but those who are opposed to the liberation of the poor and oppressed, that is, those who defend the *status quo*: the conservatives, whether they be Catholic or Protestant, Latin American or from the North. Our brothers and sisters are no longer those who belong to the same church (denomination) but those who share the same missionary point of view and fight the battle on the same side.

5. Church History in Ecumenical Perspective

T. V. Philip

Ecumenical perspective

I am firmly convinced that the way in which church history is pursued will determine the future of the nature of our Church.
(Adolf Harnack)

The church's identity is fashioned not only by its theology, ecclesiastical structure and other traditions, but also by its historians' selective interpretations of the past. The task of the church historian in every age is not only to discover new facts but also to discover new ways of thinking about them. The ecumenical perspective is the new way of thinking about the church in our time.

Ecumenism is a much wider term than is commonly understood. The ecumenical perspective does not necessarily mean the perspective of the World Council of Churches or of the Vatican Secretariat for Christian Unity. The *New Catholic Encyclopedia* defines the ecumenical movement as a developing process of inter-church relations and attitudes, the aim of which is to overcome divisions among Christians and to attain the fullness of unity in one holy, catholic and apostolic church. This is a faith-and-order approach to ecumenism and one which is commonly held in the churches. Ecumenism calls for a wider understanding of the church than is held at present in the context of its mission in the contemporary world, of its unity in relation to humankind as a whole. It calls for dialogue with other religions and spiritual traditions and incorporates the perspectives of the poor, of women, and the oppressed in its own perspective. It is this wider and more comprehensive ecumenism we are referring to in this paper.

Ecumenism does not simply mean worldwide, nor does it refer to a kind of internationalism without any local identity or roots in the situation. Ecumenism, like catholicity, means wholeness and it speaks of an inner quality. The church is ecumenical not simply because it is worldwide and unites all local churches into one organization, but because it expresses an inner wholeness, a quality of life. It is said that for the Hindu salvation means the individual soul merging with the Ultimate Reality like a drop of water merging in the great ocean and thus losing its separate identity. But for the Buddhist, according to Nancy Wilson Ross, the image should not be the drop of water which merges but rather the ocean which enters into the drop.[1] The ecumenical perspective is more like the ocean coming into a drop of water. It is the expansion of our consciousness and the widening of the horizon of our vision. It is not the loss of our identity but an enrichment of it. It is not a kind of internationalism where "local" is submerged under the "international" and which speaks of "centre" and "primacy" existing elsewhere.

In 1979 we had in India a consultation on biblical hermeneutics. At that consultation it was suggested that as Christians interested in the study of scriptures, we should also consider how the Hindu scholars interpret the Hindu scriptures. This is what we said:

> When the Indian Christians seek to understand how scriptural hermeneutics is pursued in, say, Hinduism or Buddhism, we do not do it for academic curiosity. ... We have a genuine desire to fuse our horizon with the horizon of our neighbours and see how they experience and live by their scriptures. We want to break through the walls that divide our horizon from our neighbour's in order to enlarge our own mind and to enter into a genuine two-way communication with our neighbours.[2]

This is what we mean by ecumenical perspective.

According to Hancock, an Australian historian, perspective is an alternative name for span. He says: "The historian who lacks perspective resembles a traveller who enters unknown territory with no other guide than an inch-to-mile map. The moment his journey brings him into the territory which the map does not cover, he will be lost. Perspective is both longitudinal and lateral: it places objects of immediate and intense study in its proper relationships — of time, space and theme — with other objects, near or far, which enlarge and illuminate its meaning."[3]

In 1972, when the Indian church celebrated the 1900th anniversary of the martyrdom of St Thomas, a book entitled *Christianity in India: a History in Ecumenical Perspective* was published to commemorate the occasion. In the concluding chapter of the book, I wrote then:

> Till recently the church in India has been understood in terms of Western missionary expansion. The church historians are only beginning to recognize the fact that while foreign missions have played an important role in its life and growth, the history of the Indian church is best understood as an independent story. Whether we accept the St Thomas traditions concerning the apostolic foundation of the Indian church or not, there is no doubt that the history of the church goes back to an early period. This history from an early period of Christian era up to the present is the common possession of all Christians in India. The history of Christianity in any part of India is an integral part of the history of the church anywhere in the country. Western missions which came at different periods are only different streams which have flowed in to form one main stream of Christianity in India, and they should be seen within the common tradition and not as separate traditions. It is very unfortunate that what has been written so far is only denominational histories. The denominational approach to history is essentially a communalistic approach, and not a catholic one. If we isolate events or segments from the whole, we miss the common identity that comes from the study of the whole. The history of the church in India is much larger and richer than our denominational histories, whether Roman Catholic, Protestant or Orthodox. The Indian church has a history and tradition of its own. This understanding of the unity of history is essential to maintain the integrity and wholeness of the Indian church.
>
> Church history is not simply a study of the church as a religious institution isolated from the world around. It is the history of a people's corporate response to the challenges of the gospel and their living and growing in constant dialogue with the religions and cultural situations in India.[4]

Church history in ecumenical perspective: some basic considerations

Church history and mission history

The Western historians treated the history of the churches in Asia or Africa not as independent stories but only as part of the history of Western missionary societies or missionary expansion. The churches in Asia or Africa were only dots in the missionary atlas. The definition of the church in the mission field made by the World Missionary Conference at Edinburgh, 1910, reflected the thinking of the missionary societies for a long time. Speaking of the two features of the church in the mission field, the conference report stated:

> On the one hand it is surrounded by a non-Christian community whom it is its function to subdue for the kingdom, and on the other hand, it is in close relation with an older Christian community from which it at first received the truth, which stands to it in a parental relation and still offers to it such help, leadership and even control, as may seem appropriate to the present stage of its development. ... In some smaller fields the whole population has been completely gathered into the Christian fellowship that no non-Christian community remains outside, and in some the early relation of mother and daughter church has practically merged into sisterhood, the younger church no longer being dependent for the maintenance of its activities on the older. This stage may not be capable of precise definition, but when it is fully reached the younger may be regarded as passing out of the domain of "mission" and its future course lies in the region of general church history. [5]

The missionary histories were often written from this point of view. "Triumphalism" was the note of missionary histories as well as that of colonial histories. Just as the colonial histories tried to glorify the achievements of the colonial governments, the missionary historians exaggerated the achievements of the Western missions and minimized or ignored the contributions of the churches in Africa or Asia.

For example, it is a dogma of the missionary historians that the Western missionary movement was the originator of the modern ecumenical movement. The missionary historians cite as evidence for their contention the missionary conferences in the "mission fields" where unity questions were raised in the nineteenth century and which finally led to Edinburgh and thus to the modern ecumenical movement. This is only partially true. A study of the history of the church in India and China will show that the real impetus for Christian unity came from the Indian and Chinese Christians and not from the Western missions. It was the protest of the Indian Christians against Western denominationalism and Western missionary paternalism that led to church unity discussions in some of the missionary conferences in India. Moreover, several experiments in church union were made in India in the nineteenth century by Indian Christians. The inspiration for such ecumenical initiatives came not from the Western missionary movement but from the Indian national movement.

Another sad result of treating Asian or African churches as part of the history of Western missionary expansion was that these churches did not develop a self-identity of their own and were often burdened with Western ecclesiastical problems. The solutions to these problems were also dictated along Western lines. As a result, V. Chakkarai, an Indian Christian, had to write:

> The mission field is not a fit scene where to fight out the battles of Western ecclesiasticism. They ought to be transferred to Rome, Canterbury or Geneva which is their native habitat. Strange that they should try to impose a Western solution of Western controversies on an Eastern mind. It is our tragedy that such experiments should be made on our quivering flesh. [6]

When the identity and the history of large groups of Christians are not recognized or ignored, then the whole understanding of the universality of the church is completely distorted. It was in recognizing this problem that John Garrett, the Pacific church historian, said: "Historians have an obligation to sit where Asian, African, Latin American, Caribbean and Oceanian Christians sit, to view the one church of God through their eyes and properly evaluate liturgical and theological forms of expression. The past of the whole people of God will then necessarily fall into a different total shape."[7]

The Basle consultation on church history in ecumenical perspective rightly pointed out that the distinction made between church history and the history of missions is a questionable one and that it is impossible in this way to communicate any real awareness of the universality of the church. If a church history in an ecumenical perspective is to be achieved, we must work for the integration of the two disciplines.[8]

The church as people

There is a correlation between the model of the church we hold and the way we approach church history. For a long time, the church has been identified with the clerical order and the history of the church has been understood as the history of the ecclesiastical institutions. There were times when the history of the church was identified with the history of popes and of the clerical order. The task of the historian and the theologian, as Avery Dulles points out, was to find in scripture and apostolic tradition "things that honest scholarship can scarcely find in them — such as papal-episcopal form of government, the seven sacraments, and the modern dogmas such as the Immaculate Conception and Assumption".[9] This could also be said about Protestants and Protestant historians.

An important result of the modern ecumenical discussion is the rediscovery of the church as people and that the history of the church is necessarily, in the first place, the history of the people as subjects of their own history. As stated earlier, church history is not simply a study of the church as a religious institution isolated from the world around. It is the history of a people's corporate response to the challenges of the gospel and their living and growing in constant dialogue with the religions and cultural situations in which they live.[10] Renato Constantino, a Filipino historian, describes the history of the people thus:

> History then, is the recorded struggle of the people for ever-increasing freedom and for newer and higher realizations of the human person. But the struggle is a collective one and as such involves the mass of human beings who are therefore the motivators of change and history. History is not merely a chronology of events; it is not the story of heroes and great men. Essentially, history consists of the people's efforts to attain a better life. The common people possess the capacity to make history. In fact, the historic initiative of the masses has time and again produced social cataclysms that have changed the world.[11]

In June 1985 there was a Pacific History Association conference in Suva, Fiji. In his opening address, Ratu David Toganivalu, then Deputy Prime Minister in Fiji, pointed out:

> The facts of history concern people, how they lived, what were their customs and usages, where they came from. So much evidence of these facts came only from oral traditions told in the language of the people. But, of course, it is not only language. Atmosphere, environment, relationships all play a part in getting at facts which would either be forgotten

or else perhaps considered irrelevant or unimportant. I was particularly fortunate in having a grandfather whose name I was proud to bear, who took great interest in the past and was able to act as a link between the past and the future. History is not merely a record of facts or the search for them. The events themselves are history. ... A keen attunement to custom and tradition can often enable a careful enquirer to elicit or interpret information in a way that is denied to others. There is in such tradition and custom an element of spirituality, and this can be the right wave length, not only in conversation, but in seeking to understand dances and ceremonies, songs and games. [12]

After pointing out that the history taught in the Pacific was set in an imperial rather than a Pacific context and was only of peripheral interest to the people in the Pacific, he said: "But to us in the Pacific, history is a living thing. It embodies the essence of our past and rationalizes our present." [13]

Both Constantino and Toganivalu have raised questions which are of great importance for writing and teaching church history in an ecumenical perspective. History is a living thing, speaks from and to the context of the people and speaks about things which are central to the life of the people. It tells the story of the people and reflects the experiences of the different sections of the people – of women, blacks, Aborigines, migrants, minority groups, of those who are oppressed and marginalized. Its sources are not always written records nor can it always be expressed in written language.

One of the things that impressed me at the Nairobi Assembly of the World Council of Churches was the attention given to the "disabled" in the Faith and Order discussion on unity. No unity is worth considering if it does not reflect the experience and unity of all people including the disabled. According to a group of Korean theologians, people (minjung) are the permanent reality of history. Kingdoms, dynasties and states rise and fall but the minjung (the people) remain as a concrete reality in history, dynamic, complex and changing, whose identity and reality are known through their own stories which they themselves create and therefore can tell best. [14] If so, can the church which is the koinonia of the people define itself in terms of inherited structures, hierarchy, dogma and symbols? Is church history then the history of ecclesiastical hierarchy and institutional structures which reduces the story of the people into an appendix to their history?

Today there is a growing number of ecumenically committed church groups throughout the world which are on the frontiers, struggling for the rights of the people and social justice, engaged in inter-religious dialogue and cooperation and seeking for a genuine human community in an alienated world. Their stand goes beyond the ecclesiological understandings of traditional churches to those deeper human realities of sin, suffering and alienation. According to M. M. Thomas, these groups provide a pervasive sign of hope for the community of tomorrow, and are a real — if partial — realization of the ecumenical vision of the una sancta. [15] How can the church historians come to grips with the process of self-definition of the church that is taking place in and through the work of such groups? To speak of ecumenical perspective is to raise radical questions about the nature of the church and its history.

Confessional versus ecumenical perspective

The denominational or confessional approach to history is essentially a communalistic and not a catholic one. It is a distortion of history, exaggerated and often triumphalistic. In the world map in the Scandinavian airlines' brochure, Stockholm is the centre of the world. It is a distorted view of reality. Listen to this from Letty M. Russell:

> At the beginning of 1984, the First Congregational Church of West Haven, Connecticut, got its first impulse of the new Peter's map of the world. This map shows the oceans and the continents in a different perspective because it has been drawn to show all areas according to their actual size. The church was having a family night pot luck supper and the speaker was Thomas Paton. ... He pointed to the Peter's map and asked: "What is different about this map?" A little kindergarten boy spoke up: "Russia is not cut in half." At the age of five he was already used to seeing maps with the United States in the middle and Russia divided on either side. All of us are accustomed to maps that focus on our particular self-interest. [16]

Rupert E. Davies, a Methodist historian from Britain, speaks of the Methodist preoccupation with Methodism. He says: "No other denomination spends so much time and energy in extolling its own virtues and elucidating its distinctive contributions! There seems to be a nagging fear they will be overlooked or rejected." He speaks of several historical reasons for such preoccupation of the Methodists with Methodism and then adds: "But historical reasons do not wholly excuse theological narrowness in the past; still, do they justify its continuance in the present and into the future?" [17]

The Basle consultation on church history in ecumenical perspective pointed out that the distinctiveness of every part of the church must be taken seriously, which means refusing to contrast the glories of one's own tradition with the blots of another tradition, but rather viewing both the lights and shadows of the past as our common heritage. [18]

How are we to overcome confessional distortions and express our common history as Christians? This is the main question facing us as ecumenical historians. As we stated earlier, if we isolate events or segments from the whole, we miss the common identity that comes from the study of the whole. Our common history as Christians is much larger and richer than our denominational histories, whether Roman Catholic, Protestant or Orthodox. An ecumenical perspective means taking seriously the unity of our common history. How do we achieve this?

According to Davies, one serious defect in denominational thinking is a certain pseudo-historicism. While denominations believe that God is active in history and the Holy Spirit is at all times guiding the church into all truth, they proceed to pick out certain periods in history where they think that God worked hardest and the Holy Spirit was most illuminating and thus canonize that period to the neglect of other periods. For example, the Orthodox select the period of the Great Ecumenical Councils, the Roman Catholics the high Middle Ages and the Lutherans the life and times of Martin Luther. The norms and thought and conduct of each denomination, though claimed to be based on the New Testament teaching, are really fixed by the interpretations of the New Testament in these canonical periods and their writers. While it is not wrong to attend to the utterances and examples of our fathers-in-faith, "it is purely absurd to suggest that God's work or revelation in one period of history takes precedence over what he does and says in other periods", [19] except at the time of incarnation. It is interesting that the Methodists who do not accept the succession of a particular ministry through the episcopal laying on of hands are found canonizing the sermons and notes on the New Testament of John Wesley and even the doctrinal clauses of the Deed of Union of 1932.

"The truth is that denominational loyalty, leading to the desire to preserve the faith and disciplines of one's own church, has come to obscure the fact that Sermons and Notes and the Deed are historical documents — just as the Roman Catholic Church has taken four difficult centuries to see that the decrees of the Council of Trent are historical documents."[20] The historical documents are written in a particular historical context in answer to particular historical problems and under particular pressures. This does not mean that we ignore or discredit these documents. Davies explains that a clear distinction must be made between the form in which a statement is made where the historical context is highly operative, and the context of the statement where the historical context is still certainly operative but in a different way. Once this is made, it becomes the business of the theologian and the historian to disentangle, first of all, the form and the content and then within the content the relative and the absolute, that which belongs to the time of writing and that which is permanently true if it is true at all.[21]

The confessional approach to history is that it very often gives normative status to a particular historical period, event or person. A study of history should help us to transcend the accident of history and to be creative in the present. This will be possible only if the persons, events and statements of the past are seen in their historical context so that what is temporary can be disentangled from what is permanent. The study of church history in ecumenical perspective means that history becomes a point of liberation from the burdens of the past. It should help the churches to ensure that the legacies of quarrels now irrelevant should not impede our coming together.

Not only should we see the events and persons in their wider historical context, but we should also see them in relation to one another and not as isolated events: for example, recent Luther studies by Roman Catholic historians in the wider context of the history of the sixteenth century and in relation to the development both in the Protestant world and the Catholic Church have brought about a new understanding of Luther. Indeed, Daniel Olivier, the French Roman Catholic historian, has come to see the Protestant Reformation as complementary to the Catholic Reformation in the sixteenth century, and could write: "The time has come also for the exodus of the churches from confessional securities towards the promised land of evangelical communion. ... It is time to bring to an end a thousand years of history, to throw off the narrowness and self-sufficiency which has marked our confessional allegiance, and deliberately to turn ourselves to the future."[22]

The task of the church historian is to place facts in the wider context of secular history and also in relation to one another. Raimundo Panikkar makes an observation which is of the utmost importance to our subject of discussion. He points out that Christian ecumenism, if it is really to be ecumenical, cannot be reduced to settling Christian family feuds, as it were, or healing old wounds. It has also to take into account the entire world situation and try to find the place of the religions of the world in this "Christian Economy of Salvation", without a priori subordination of other religions to the Christian self-understanding. Panikkar goes on to say: "A by-product of this ecumenical attitude is that it affords the best setting for the right perspective, even in merely Christian controversies. Catholics and Protestants would more easily discover their different contexts and understand each other more fully, for instance, when dealing with the nature of the sacraments, if they tried to understand also the nature of the Hindu Samskaras, instead of arguing only from their respective standpoints. ... It is when seen against a wider and common horizon that divergences and common perspectives appear."[23] The ecumenical perspective is this wider and common horizon and it is the task of the church historian to provide it.

Global perspective

We have stated earlier that ecumenism does not refer to a kind of internationalism without any local identity. At the present time, there is a large number of people who are advocates of a certain kind of internationalism and the concept of the "one world". Anwar M. Barkat of Pakistan, speaking of the socio-political considerations in relation to the unity of the church and the unity of humankind, points out that multinational corporations look upon themselves as the champions of one world and the emerging world of interdependence. They have only contempt for the modern nation state and consider themselves to be the means of dissemination of technical know-how, capital and production. "To those who are victims of multinational corporations, they are expressions of a new form of imperialism and colonialism." Barkat says:

> It is a fact that Western culture and Western churches have been interdependent. The wealth of the Western churches is not unrelated to the wealth of the Western nations. The centrality of the Western churches is mainly due to their political dominance in modern history. Since there is a parallelism between Western churches and Western nations, how will this be transcended for the unity of the church? Or will the unity of the church be met in terms and conditions dictated by Western churches and Western civilization?[24]

Barkat has raised a serious issue for the ecumenical movement. No discussion of the universality and oneness of the church is of any use unless we recognize the forces and factors that affect international life today. In the West, there exists strong and economically powerful churches, confessional families and "crusading organizations" which claim universal supremacy and responsibility. In ecumenical discussions in the West, questions of "centre" and "primacy" are often raised. Ecumenical perspective is not the internationalism of the multinational corporations. It takes the local situation seriously. Alan Richardson points out that the fact of "locality" is an important aspect of the New Testament doctrine of the church. "The church is not like a school of Stoic philosophers whose existence in a given place is quite accidental. The Catholic Church is always a local church, the church of some city or country.... Locality, nationality and particularity are the essential marks of the universal church."[25] Richardson goes on to say that the opposite of universal is not local but denominational. The ecumenical perspective must be one which is well informed about developments throughout the world, through research, study and mutual sharing. It means a large number of local and regional studies.

However, "local" does not mean "parochial". Confessionalism and parochialism are two evils which distort the vision of the historian. President Shriver of the Union Theological Seminary was aware of this when he wrote:

> Generally church leaders know a confessional form of theology that generally supports their holding on to the status quo, whereas more historical theology shows the ups and downs of Christianity through the centuries and better prepares the church for change.... Until 1960, it was possible for a person to feel himself or herself well educated in this

society and never to have paid any attention to what we now call the third world. You did not really have to know anything about Africa or Latin America or the Pacific or Asia. You studied "The Tradition" defined culturally as the Atlantic or Mediterranean community.[26]

Past is living

Ecumenical perspective means that historians must make the past alive, and bring it to bear on the ecumenical issues and problems we face today. A number of the issues and problems we face today are not entirely new. Similar questions were raised in the past, though in different contexts and in different ways. We cannot completely identify past issues with those of the present and apply past solutions. Though not identical, some of the ecumenical issues being faced today have a striking similarity with some of the issues faced by the church earlier. One example from the history of the early church is the way that the Jew and Gentile controversy helps us to understand the nature of the catholicity of the church. The early church understood the catholicity of its nature and message in confrontation with and apart from the ethnic homogeneity of Palestinian Judaism. It was something like a "discovery" while the church was engaged in mission. Similarly, the present-day churches will be catholic to the extent that race, colour, caste and national prejudices and segregations are historically conquered and separations based on them are done away with in the life of the churches. The history of the early church teaches us that catholicity is not a status symbol safeguarded by ecclesiastical structure; it is primarily a relationship and a task. It emerges in mission and manifests itself in the openness of the church to humanity in Christ. The history of the early church shows that issues of ecumenism and the unity of the church are much deeper and wider than what is involved in simply amalgamating Anglican and Methodist ecclesiastical structures into one. The issues in ecumenism are rooted in the issues of humanity itself.

To take another example, the Donatist movement in North Africa in the fourth century had radically raised the place of economic and political factors in the divisions of the church and the importance of these factors in our search for unity. What we notice in this controversy between the Catholic (Latin) Church and the Donatists was that the Empire and the Emperor, the Latin Catholic Church and the rich landlords were on one side and the nationalists, the Donatists and the exploited poor on the other. The Latin church in North Africa was a colonial church largely linked with one particular class, one particular language and one particular culture. It was the church of the Romans, supporting the interest of the well-to-do and the ruling class. W. H. C. Frend mentions that Roman society found its last interpreters in the Catholic bishops. The Donatists drew their strength largely from the poor peasants and the middle class, economically, politically and religiously exploited by foreigners. Though at the beginning issues raised were about the holiness of the church and the validity of the sacraments, the issues involved were much more than that. Frend points out that the history of the Donatist movement makes it clear that politics, economics, geography and culture are important factors, sometimes more so than purely dogmatic questions in the history of the division and unity of the church. He sums up his study of Donatism thus:

> Donatism and Catholicism represented two opposite tendencies in early Christian thought. The churches were in fact two societies, differing fundamentally in outlook on both religious and social questions. Did the Catholics refer to the purity of the sacraments or to the extent of the church over the inhabited world? Was the church within the Roman empire

sustaining and sustained by the Christian Emperors, or was the empire representative of the outer world, whence the Christian must separate himself in order to progress in faith? Were social evils and injustices to be fought in the name of Christ, or were they to be tolerated for the sake of Christian unity? To all these questions, the Donatists and the Catholics gave different answers. The issues were not those of "truth" versus "heresy" but of two opposed attitudes to society, attitudes which have persisted throughout the history of the Christian church down to the present day.[27]

Does unity mean that we should tolerate injustice and exploitation in church and society? The history of the Donatist movement radically raises this question for the church's search for unity.

Christian identity: our common history as Christians

Maurice Wiles, the Oxford Patristic scholar,[28] speaking of the relevance of traditions of the early church for our time, points out that the essence of historical consciousness in our day is that we are all, in one degree or another, historical relativists. That means, we recognize the need to assess all statements in relation to the particular situations of the time. For example, the dogmatic utterances of the early church councils emerged out of the broader theological debates of their own time and cannot simply be taken straight out of their original setting and transplanted into the soil of modern theological affirmations. But this does not mean that historical consciousness has no positive implications. It insists that the present cannot be properly understood without reference to the past. An attempt to understand how we have emerged from the past and reached the position in which we now stand is a part of the process of interpreting our present situation. The church cannot ignore any aspects of its past; theology must be concerned with church history as a whole.[29]

Wiles raises the question of identity. "By what criteria are we to judge if we stand in a true succession to the church of earlier generations?"[30] In other words, what is the essence of our Christian tradition? According to him, the test of identity cannot be located in any specific isolatable elements of Christian belief or practice. We cannot say in advance of any particular tenet that it is and always will be a test of the true church. Continuity can be expressed not only by the continued presence of specific elements; it can also be expressed by a kind of family likeness which may persist even when there is a change in respect of each individual item involved. It is surely identity of this kind for which we should look in the life of the church. "It will be difficult to know when we have it and impossible to be certain. But is it not the kind of continuity and identity that is appropriate to the realm of the Spirit?"[31] At a time when ecumenical discussion on continuity and tradition is based on common belief and ecclesiastical structures, it is refreshing to hear a different point of view.

If the early church understood the catholicity of its nature in confrontation with and demarcation from ethnic homogeneity of Palestinian Judaism, it understood the nature of the universality of the gospel in its confrontation and dialogue with Greco-Roman culture. It was a discovery for the early church as it engaged in mission. The Jews had a negative attitude to all that was pagan, as they believed that God had elected them to be an exclusive nation uncorrupted by heathen influences. The first Christians, being Jews, shared the Jewish attitude to pagans and Roman society in general. When the church crossed the boundaries of Palestinian Judaism and entered into the wider area of the Greco-Roman world, it found itself in the midst of a religiously and culturally pluralistic society and the question of the church's relation to pagan society and culture became a crucial theological one. The attitude of Christians in general to pagan polytheism and idol worship was absolutely negative. But a creative encounter took place between Christianity and Greek culture and philosophy. In this there was no one tradition universally followed by all Christians. While Tatian took a negative attitude, Justin Martyr was very positive in his evaluation of Greek philosophy. Justin defined the identity of Christianity as a school of philosophy and wrote: "Christ is the logos of whom every race of men partakes and those who live rationally are Christians even if thought to be atheists.... Whatever things have been rightly said by any one belongs to us Christians."[32] Clement of Alexandria believed that the idea of God is implanted in all people at creation. There is a spark of nobility in every soul which is kindled by the divine logos. All wisdom is summed up in Christ who is the Uniting Principle. " There is the one river of truth, but many streams fall into it on this side and that." Some Christians of Clement's day, who criticized Greek philosophy, argued that Greek philosophy was stolen from Moses or from heaven as Prometheus stole fire. Against them Clement asked: "Is not fire beneficial? We must always judge by what is said, not by who said it."[33]

Because of this positive attitude, the church fathers were able to use Greek philosophy and culture not only to express Christian faith but also for a deeper understanding of it. In its encounter with Greek culture, the church no longer understood itself as a Jewish sect living in a Semitic milieu, but a universal religion which can find its home in all cultures. It was in its missionary encounter with Greco-Roman culture that the church grasped the universalism of the gospel, which made it possible for the church to express itself in all cultures and in all particular situations. It finds its own form and expression in each situation and in each age. Harnack, in a significant statement, points out:

> But the reasons for the triumph of Christianity in that age are no guarantee for the permanence of that triumph throughout the history of mankind. Such a triumph rather depends on the simple elements of religion, on the preaching of the living God as the Father of men and on the likeness of Jesus Christ. For that very reason it depends upon the capacity of Christianity to strip off once more any collective syncretism and unite itself to fresh co-efficients. [34]

To be universal therefore means a plurality of Christian expressions in structure and theology. Plurality is something inbuilt in the very nature of the church because it is an element of the gospel itself. J. Danielou points out:

> The transition of the religion of Christ from the Jewish world, within which it made its first appearance, to the pagan world is the great revolution that occupies the first and second centuries. This was the natural outcome of the very nature of the Christian message, which is not the religious expression of culture, as were the great pagan religions, and not the election by God of one people for an historic mission, as was Judaism, but is the proclamation to all mankind of the advent of the last things. [35]

The preaching of the gospel in each generation and in each situation, the ability of the gospel to find its expression in each culture and in each situation and the manifestation of the catholic nature of the church in terms of its demarcation from the demons of class, race, colour and national prejudices both in church and society and its ability to create fellowship transcending these natural divisions — all these are basic elements of traditions of the church and therefore our common Christian heritage. Our common history is the history of how the universality of the gospel and the catholicity of the church are manifested in each age and in each situation. Both catholicity and universality are not static qualities which can be expressed by institutional structures or structures of theology. They are dynamic qualities and can be expressed or manifested in the church's mission as it lives in constant dialogue with the world.

The Christian church has a tradition of its own. But an essential element in the church's tradition is the work of the Holy Spirit in unfolding the universality of the gospel and the catholicity of the nature of the church in each generation and in each situation.

To speak of church history in ecumenical perspective is to speak of this tradition of universality and catholicity. It will be a colourful story and can be best expressed by people themselves in their own way. Like Maurice Wiles, we may also ask whether this is not the kind of ecumenical history that is appropriate to the realm of the Spirit.

NOTES

[1] *Buddhism: a Way of Life and Thought*, Collins, 1981.
[2] Unpublished report of the consultation.
[3] W. K. Hancock, *Perspective in History*, Canberra, ANU, 1982, p.vii.
[4] H. C. Perumalil ed., *Christianity in India*, Prakasam Publications, Appelley, 1972, pp.300-301.
[5] *The Church in the Mission Field* (World Missionary Conference, 1910), Edinburgh, 1910, p.5.
[6] D. M. Devasahayam ed., *Rethinking Christianity in India*, Madras, 1938, p.282.
[7] Lukas Vischer ed., *Church History in an Ecumenical Perspective*, Bern, 1982, p.59.
[8] *Ibid.*, p.114.
[9] *Models of the Church*, New York, Doubleday & Company Inc., 1978, p.49.
[10] See T. V. Philip in *Christianity in India*, p.300.
[11] *The Philippines*, pp.5-6 (quoted in *Religion and Society*, Bangalore, 1980, pp.10-11).
[12] In *Pacific History Association Newsletter*, 14, pp.5-6.
[13] *Ibid.*
[14] Kim Yong Bock, in *Minjung Theology*, Christian Conference of Asia, 1984, p.186.
[15] In *Voices of Unity*, World Council of Churches, 1981, p.100.
[16] Letty Russell ed., *Changing Contexts of our Faith*, Fortress Press, 1985, p.21.
[17] John Deschner ed., *Our Common History as Christians*, Oxford University Press, 1975, p.33.
[18] Vischer ed., *op. cit.*, p.107.
[19] Deschner ed., *op. cit.*, p.40.
[20] *Ibid.*, p.40.
[21] *Ibid.*
[22] *Luther's Faith*, St Louis, Concordia, 1982, p.167.
[23] "Towards an Ecumenical Ecumenism", *Journal of Ecumenical Studies*, fall 1982, pp.784-785.
[24] "Some Socio-political Considerations", in *Unity in Today's World*, World Council of Churches, 1978, pp.103-116.
[25] *An Introduction to the Theology of the New Testament*, London, SCM Press Ltd, 1958, pp.288-289.
[26] *The Union News*, the President's report, 1982–83, p.8.
[27] W. H. C. Frend, *The Early Church*, p.332.
[28] *Working Papers in Doctrine*, London, SCM Press Ltd, 1976, p.93.
[29] *Ibid.*, p.99.
[30] *Ibid.*, p.105.
[31] *Ibid.*, p.106.
[32] In *Second Apology*.
[33] Strom. 1:5.
[34] *The Mission and Expansion of Christianity in the First Three Centuries*, 2nd ed., Vol. 1, p.318.
[35] In *The Crucible of Christianity*, A. Toynbee ed., p.275.

6. Teaching Systematic Theology Ecumenically

Adriaan Geense

Three years ago I gave up my position as teacher of systematic theology at a university in the Netherlands that I had occupied for ten years and became responsible for the teaching of ecumenical theology at the Ecumenical Institute of Bossey. If I had taught systematic theology before in an ecumenical perspective, I now have to teach ecumenical theology in a systematic perspective. And the question is: Is there such a thing as ecumenical theology, above all places where people teach theology concretely in the context of their church and university, a discipline that you can isolate and teach at a special ecumenical place? To a similar question, as to whether the World Council of Churches is a super-church above the churches, the answer is: No. There is no such super-theology above all the concrete theologies that exist in the churches. As we can only join in the work of the World Council of Churches by being a member of our own church, so we can only join in ecumenical theology by being responsible primarily for the teaching of systematic theology in our own specific places.

By returning, however, to our own places that are more real to us, the task of relating systematic theology to an ecumenical perspective does not become easier. There are many conceptions of systematic theology and there are many different ways in which the word "ecumenical" is used. Therefore we could imagine also many possible combinations between the two key words "systematic" and "ecumenical".

But here we are helped by the formulation of our theme. We do not have to speak in an abstract way about the concept of systematic theology in a possible ecumenical perspective, but we have to deal with *teaching* systematic theology in an ecumenical perspective. And here I think that, starting from some basic observations, we can avoid falling into the trap that we set out with a very specific concept of systematic theology of which we could develop the ecumenical relevance only for those who are adherents of that concept.

Personally I prefer the term "dogmatics" to "systematic theology" as it better conveys the notion of identity of the Christian faith as something outspoken. But for our purpose we should rather start with "systematic theology".

Putting things together

Teaching systematic theology is being responsible for a process of bringing things in theology together. "Systematic" is not primarily derived from "system" into which things in theology should fit, but from the original meaning of the word *sustenai*, to put things together, to bring things into relation. This bringing together is a special activity, a special responsibility, you could call it a "specialism", a specialism sometimes despised by the specialists in the different subjects of theology, like exegesis or history.

Systematicians are often suspected by their colleagues in the faculty of not being scientific, not knowing the facts or turning the facts to the advantage of their systems. I have known an exegete in my former faculty who used to say: I produce the facts, here are the facts. What you do with them does not concern me, it is not my responsibility. Leave it to "practical theology", a discipline with a less academic reputation than the other disciplines of the theological encyclopedia. Even if it is not said so sharply, the reality in many faculties of theology is that the scientific value is measured more in the achievements in the isolated disciplines than in the concern for coherence of the different disciplines in the one and the same direction taken by the whole of the faculty. Measuring the scientific value of theology primarily by its relations to the methodology of the other disciplines at the university automatically implies an increasing degree of abstraction in relation to the concrete places where theology arises. That's why "systematic theology" has as its prime function the task of putting things, aspects, perspectives together that tend to isolate themselves.

Alan Falconer has illustrated his presentation on the significance of the main ecumenical events by introducing analogies out of the world of music. Let me give one more example out of this rich world of musical analogies. The late Dutch theologian Miskotte, who was my master for systematic theology, has compared the role of the systematic theologian, the dogmatician, with the conductor of an orchestra. In his farewell lecture to Leiden University he spoke about the systematic theologian as "dilettant" and "dirigent". Compared to the musicians in the orchestra he/she is often an amateur, but at the same time he/she is responsible for the good interplay of all the separate instruments. The conductor has the possibility of interpretation of the totality of the symphony. He/she knows the direction and can put the emphasis where he/she thinks it is good for bringing out the intention of the composer.[1]

Now as the systematic theologian has the task of bringing together the different aspects of theology that have been dealt with elsewhere in an isolated way, in the same way he/she carries responsibility for putting together the different confessional perspectives under which the isolated theologies are often treated. In our institutions of theological training we are used to distinguish denominational, interdenominational and supra-denominational schools and faculties of theology, the last category often called "department of religion", without any link to a specific church, or even to Christianity as such. We might be tempted to consider the interdenominational institutions of theology and the departments of religion as more open and ecumenical than a denominational school. This is however not necessarily the case. Some interdenominational institutions have their structure of organization only for practical or financial reasons and are not ecumenical in the bringing together of the different confessional perspectives. On the other hand it must be said that if a student is not already rooted in a denominational church and has no place of identity, the synthesis becomes more difficult. The ecumenical perspective does not arise automatically in an interdenominational setting, it is a conscious and deliberate activity that has to be brought into theology by putting things together.

This "bringing-things-together" therefore is a fundamental movement that is not something accidental, but is rooted in the essence of the gospel itself. The gospel is the message not about an isolated God, but about God opening God's very self for humankind and humankind being opened up for God and, with it, the opening up of people for fellow human beings. This fundamental movement of the bringing together of God and the human person, and the human being with other human beings, is reflected in the church, where people are brought together, assembled by the gospel. The fundamental notion in the word church, "ekklesia", is "gathering, assembling".[2] And the fundamental structure of the ecumenical movement is the assembly. From there all the other activities of the World Council of Churches are directed.

Systematic theology, therefore, in its most basic sense reflects the fundamental movement of God and the fundamental movement of the church in bringing things together. It is a counter-movement to the fundamental movement of sin; the refusal to be in communion, the striving for self-sufficiency. This sin is also extended to the churches, as they try to live for themselves. If they organize theology in such a way that its aim is to state what distinguishes one church from the others, then it becomes theology of controversy: as the German expression runs, *sich mit jemandem auseinandersetzen*: to put yourself at a distance from somebody. Doing systematic theology in an ecumenical perspective is to decide not to do theology any longer without the other, not to take a distance from them because of some apparent mistakes and weaknesses, not to expose them, but take up responsibility also for the other's weaknesses. Systematic theology is theology that organizes an encounter and is willing to integrate the results of that encounter into its own thinking. In the same way as the gospel has to be brought and taught to us, because we do not know it by ourselves, systematic theology has to be brought and taught to us, because we do not do it by ourselves in an ecumenical perspective.

Systematic theology designed by the precedence of the encounter over against the self-contained existence reminds us of another fundamental structure of theology, the precedence of the *spoken* word over against the *written* theology. Theologians say: I have *written* a systematic theology. You can see the system only by having patience and reading the whole book and letting the composition speak to you. The order and the coherence and the logic are essential for the disposition. The coherence is in the mind of the author.

We have to remember, however, that theology had its origin in the spoken word, not in the written word. The writing down of the gospel was a second phase, and remains linked with the primary function of the spoken word. The writing down is only to make a future speaking possible. The gospel is proclamation. It directs itself to persons and provokes an answer. The apostle Paul is not liked by some Christians because they consider him as the first systematic theologian of the church to write dogmatic treatises. This is not true: what we have received from Paul are not treatises, but letters. A letter is a moment in the dialogue, that takes temporarily another form because of the absence of the speaking partner, but having still the same structure of dialogue. The address is the first part of the letter. The name of the partner in dialogue is mentioned. The letter wants to provoke response, and appeals to the reader. There are several places where even in a so-called treatise, the argumentative style that wants to convince the other comes up in expressions like: "Don't you know that..." (Rom.

6:3; 7:1, 1 Cor. 5:6; 6:2,15). The oldest form of the written gospel — before our so-called gospels were written — was the Pauline letter which has a dialogical character.

With the shift from the spoken to the written word, a shift of structure is possible that makes systematic theology lose its dialogical character. In the Middle Ages systematic theology was developed in disputes, where every thesis was countered by an anti-thesis, *sic* and *non*. The Reformation began with the publication of the 95 theses of Luther that were meant for public dispute. The form-principle of both the Summa Theologica of Thomas Aquinas and the Heidelberg Catechism is that of *question* and *answer*.[3] That means that even in its written form, theology did not want to forget its origin in the dialogue and that it cannot be done alone.

Of course it is possible that a written theology preserves a dialectical, dialogical structure. The most famous example of our time is, in my opinion, Karl Barth's *Church Dogmatics*, against the impression it gives of a closed systematic construction, a building without a door as it has been called. In essence, however, it is a most open system, in continuous conversation with scripture, with the fathers of the early church, with the Reformers, with contemporary philosophers and theologians looking for communion with those who before us have heard, explained and confessed the gospel, and written in the service of a renewed proclamation of the word.

So the assembling, putting things together, organizing a dialogue is the first and fundamental structure of a systematic theology in ecumenical perspective. To be a teacher in this operation means being called and put under the obligation to organize and present the maximum number of different perspectives. Of course the practice of our daily work imposes natural limitations. Even in an age of global interdependence it is not easy to organize theological work that breaks away from the situation of the homogeneity of place and confession. Our Ecumenical Institute in Bossey tries, by its policy of scholarships, to break through this starting condition of any theological enterprise by organizing the encounter with the largest number of differences in viewpoint and perspectives. In this way, and looking at our analysis of the primary structures of doing ecumenical theology, we could call Bossey the highest possible form of "systematic theology". We should remember, however, what was said before about Bossey as an extra-territorial place, where not *a* situation, *a* context characterizes the work, but the attempt to organize a market, an exchange-place, and that the very fact of realizing such places makes us conscious of the necessity to start from local allegiances.

But we should not idealize situations like Bossey or the WCC assemblies over against the regular places where systematic theology is produced. In going back to the original sense of the word "systematic" and relating it to the fundamental movement of "assembling" we stated the precedence of the dialogue and oral theology over against written theology. But neither the World Council nor Bossey can escape the obligations of writing things down. It should be clear, however, that in the same way as the process of the writing down of scripture serves for speaking in the future, the World Council's written publications should serve as a basis for new encounters. There has been a fair amount of enthusiasm over the production of a convergence text on "Baptism, Eucharist and Ministry". It was even said that it was a product of a dialogue that had gone on for fifty years. It went through several stages of asking the churches' contributions to it. And now that the "final" stage has been reached, the World Council again has asked the churches for "reception". What else can that mean except that the ongoing process of participation in the discussion is considered to be more important than the fixing of a so-called final stage in a text? Here we should remember the words of Ernst Lange: "People struggling together to find the truth are so much more interesting and produce so much more of truth than the protocols of the truces and the peace treaties they write."[4]

Neither should we be silent about the only place where Bossey occurs in the *Church Dogmatics* of Karl Barth. Speaking about the ecumenical movement he writes:

> ...It can hardly be maintained that what was said at Amsterdam or Evanston has made any great impact. Nor is the reason for this to be found merely in the necessary element of compromise in such common statements (hence the fog of indecision and sterility which envelops from the very first all the ecumenical papers so industriously prepared at Bossey and elsewhere). It is to be found also in the difficulty that as yet there has been no clear apprehension of the concrete things so earnestly sought in innumerable ecumenical conferences of students, which the church has to proclaim to the disorder of secular politics and economics as the message of salvation.[5]

Confessing Christ

All this has brought us now to a point where we have to turn to the analysis of a second basic element that should be considered in speaking about teaching systematic theology in an ecumenical perspective. In a first step we have tried to develop the ecumenical character of theology by drawing out the parallel between the original sense of "systematic": "putting things together", and the basic movement of the church: coming together, assembling. Coming together, putting things together, however, is not done for the simple pleasure of coming and putting things together; it is coming together because we have been called together by the gospel. And now it is we who have to react to that call. We have to do something with it. God has said something and now we should say something in response. We should confess that we have heard the word and that we have understood that it is the truth about our life. We should thank and praise God for the word, we should identify that word together as members of the church, and we should confess that message also to the world outside the church. All these three aspects of our reaction could be summarized in one word, "confession". In all these three aspects "confession" is the root of all theology. Theology is rooted in doxology, in the necessity of identifying and transmitting the gospel inside the church, and in the call to witness to the world outside the church. In this fundamental structure "confession" as a basis of theology can be understood by all the churches. In the call for an answer, every church becomes a "confession" in the positive sense of the word. "Assembling" and "confessing" are the two key words of theology. Once you have assembled, you confess. You say something basic and simple, like Jesus is Lord. It is the oldest Christian confession and it is the common confessional basis of the World Council of Churches.[6]

It is a confession at the beginning of the development of Christian dogma and doctrine and it is a confession to return to after a long and complicated development of dogma and doctrine that divided the Christians. But it is that long period between the beginning and our present challenge to confession that most of our systematic theology is about. In reworking that period we should make it clear that the main themes of the discussion are part of an ecumenical dialogue. This dialogue is inherent to the Christian confession, as it wants to identify the unity in the many different situations of confession in space and time. Systematic theology can only be taught and developed from a clear vision of its basic scope: the identification of the common Christian message in the variety of testimonies in scripture, in the variety of challenges with which the church was confronted as it started its way through history, in order to prepare the church for an adequate confession *now*. It has not a historical, but an actual scope.

Right from the beginning the church has assembled in its representative bodies to come to an agreement about points that had become a matter of dispute. It starts with the "apostles council" in Acts 15 and continues in the ecumenical councils of the early church. The Orthodox churches consider these as the base for any ecumenical theology. But I think we could also consider the appearance of the Reformation in the sixteenth century in all its variations and with all its predecessors in the late Middle Ages as a manifestation of a great ecumenical dialogue about the identity of the gospel. Surely a dialogue that did not reach the desired result, a dialogue that was not organized in the form of a council, but still a dialogue in which the presence of the other partner was sought, as testified by the two conferences between Catholics and Protestants, in Hagenau in 1540 and in Regensburg in 1541, before they finally parted and the Roman Catholic Church organized its own Council of Trent. The Reformation churches did not organize a Council but answered with a wealth of confessions which project the cause of the Reformation as a cause for the whole catholic church.

It is only after the Reformation that confessions had to organize themselves as separate churches. Very soon they lost the communion with each other and became used to their separate existence. The rediscovery of the centrality of justification by faith, in a situation that the practice of church life seemed to contradict it at every step, was offered by Luther as a central element of the Christian confession for reception by the whole church. Because this offering was not received by the whole church in the sense in which Luther had understood it, the Evangelical Lutheran churches had to organize their church life as a life separate from the main catholic church. Because the dialogue was refused, the contradiction to the dialogue was institutionalized in a separate church. All churches of the Reformation however did not organize their church as a protecting community around one central polemic element of Christian doctrine, but pretended that the full catholicity was in every one of their churches. It is the institutionalizing of churches around separate aspects of the Christian confession that normally should be in dialogue within the one church that causes the ecumenical problem. The separate existence of institutions causes the separate organization of theology. Of course there is no reason for the separate existence of the Lutherans for the defence of representation of the doctrine of justification. As such the unity concept of "reconciled diversity" that is developed in Lutheran circles cannot be the last word. It is not as defenders of one article of faith that Lutherans participate in the ecumenical dialogue, but because of the fact that their separate existence as a church cannot abrogate the claim that they make together with others to be truly catholic.

It is often said in defence of the existence of separate churches that "truth" should prevail above unity. If a person or a group rediscovers a central aspect of the Christian message at a place where that has been forgotten and that aspect is not integrated, this "truth" or confession becomes institutionalized as a "confession" or a denomination. The institutionalization of these elements of truth implies automatically that they lose their character of elements in dialogue, their capacity of systematization in the good sense of the word of being "put together", being assembled. Teaching systematics in an ecumenical perspective will mean then to take up teaching responsibility, against all institutional allegiance, for investigating the Christian faith in its capacity to create community and unity. Truth and unity in the biblical sense are not contradictions or two entities that can tolerate each other only with some difficulty.

Again one can look at the character of Pauline theology, that often is considered to be dogmatic, in the sense of anti-thetic and polemic. In reality his life-long theological activity can be characterized as the continuous concern for the discovery of theological viewpoints that can unite the different parts of the people of God: beginning with the unity between Israel and the church, continuing with the different groups in the church of Corinth that all boast to have an apostolic name, and ending with the doxology of love that unites and transcends all the different charismata that tend to work against each other instead of with each other (1 Cor. 13).

Teaching systematic theology in ecumenical perspective therefore is being thoroughly convinced of the uniting capacity of the Christian truth, and to investigate that capacity with all the scientific, exegetical, historical and philosophical tools at our disposal. The question of truth remains central. Being an ecumenical systematical theologian does not mean being a relativist. It does not mean the rejection of doctrine as a dividing factor in favour of life and work as uniting factors. Unity is the ecclesial form of truth.

The Roman Catholic decree on ecumenism offers as help for the ecumenical discussion the concept of the hierarchy of truths (*hierarchia veritatum*).[7] It is offered with the expectation that by the establishment of such a hierarchy among the "truths" that are the cause for doctrinal and ecclesial separation, we possess a method of deciding whether the different points of dissension still possess sufficient weight and importance to justify the ongoing separate existence of the churches. The difficulty with this concept is that Christian doctrine cannot be divided quantitatively. The last perspective of the Christian doctrine is not a plurality of "truths", but the truth who is a Person: Jesus Christ. And the dialogue should continue as far as to reach him. It may be argued, for instance, that differences in the conception of ministry in the last resort came down to a different understanding of Christ and his work.[8] The ecumenical dialogue should not stop at the establishment of a hierarchy of "truths" but be permitted to penetrate into that last perspective.

The proposition of the concept of confession as the basic structure of the response of the church after it has been assembled by the gospel, and as a basic element of recognition, has yet another advantage. As it lies, so to speak, still before the development of doctrine, it can engage also those churches in the ecumenical perspective that have not developed an elaborate relation to doctrine, or have even constituted themselves in a conscious refusal of any explicit doctrine or theologizing that they consider to be at the basis of church disunity. The Salvation Army and many Pentecostal churches for instance have hardly developed any doctrine, but have at the same time a strong confessional quality in the original sense of the word. So also the Orthodox churches, which have developed a very large doctrinal theology, but still consider this doctrine more under the doxological than under a juridical perspective that has been developed in the West. In the doxology they confess, but they do not have "confessions" as in the West, that have to legitimize their differences.

One can put this issue also as follows. The need for a developed theology is not everywhere the same. We do not have to consider every partner in the ecumenical dialogue as a potential consumer of the same quantity of theology. We should always ask what again and again provokes theology in spite of all existing theology. The challenges in which a church has to confess may differ from one situation to another. The challenge to become a confessional church was much more acute for the church in Germany during the Nazi period than for the church of Canada. The Barmen Theological Declaration developed the fundamental confession of the Lordship of Christ in a totally new actuality when others were proposing themselves as lords. The confessional situation in South Africa is much more acute than that for the church in Finland or Norway.

This does not mean that the quantity of the developed theology is in proportion to the acute character of the challenge. The Barmen Theological Declaration was a very short confession, but it was surrounded by the voluminous *Church Dogmatics* of Karl Barth, that lives on the same basic assumptions. On the other hand, the churches that gather in the World Council of Churches, the World Alliance of Reformed Churches and the Lutheran World Federation know very well that in the situation of South Africa the "status confessionis" has been reached, but there is very little elaborate theology around it.

What is important is that in none of the forms of theology, whether they have been elaborated in a classical way — in a broad discussion with exegesis, with the history of doctrine and with philosophy — or whether they operate in a more impressionistic way, the element of "now", of the "kairos", of the actuality of the confession is missing.

The purpose of doing systematic theology in an ecumenical perspective is not to relativize the sharpness of the doctrinal controversies, but to reinforce the confession of the church in an actual situation.

It is important to realize this basic structure of the link between assembling and confessing in order to understand better the World Council of Churches as a place where this link becomes operational. Just because of the fact that the WCC cannot replace any of the constituent churches, is no super-church that takes up the functions of any local church, and has no institutional continuous life in the same way as the churches, the basic structure of assembling and confessing becomes visible much earlier. It is often remarked that the WCC is an activist organization and that the theological life that is concentrated in Faith and Order is underdeveloped in relation to the many activities of which it should be the basis. Professional systematic theologians seem to prefer the bilateral theological discussions, as they are mostly organized between the great confessional traditions by the Christian World Communions and the Roman Catholic Church, to the multilateral discussions in the World Council's context, that seem to be much less precise and far too general.

Bilateral theological discussions have indeed a different structure from the assemblies and the meetings of the Central Committee of the World Council. In bilateral conversations it is not churches but representative theologians of confessional traditions that come together. They speak about the differences of confessions, but they never confess together. The assembling of churches in the World Council however immediately makes visible the unity of confession and action. With less explicit theology the confessing character does not become weaker, but stronger. In an article

"Confessing Church and Ecumene" (1935), Dietrich Bonhoeffer has witnessed from his own experience in the ecumenical movement (which at that time had not yet institutionalized in the World Council of Churches) that churches that have not yet come to full unity in a certain given situation confess together the truth of the gospel against its perversion.[9] The truth of the gospel is not guaranteed by the theoretical and theological safeguarding of the basic formula of the WCC, but only by the confessing of the Lordship of Jesus Christ in action.

Therefore we can say: the more systematic theology approaches its central theme, the confession of the Lordship of Jesus Christ, a confession from which all doctrine sprang, the less it has a need to be explicitly ecumenical. Not a concept of unity, but Jesus Christ as the only mediator between God and the human person is the unity of the church. To rediscover this is the basis of what has been called the Copernican revolution[10] in theology that before was organized by the confessions. It consists in the decision not to look any longer at other confessions as if they move around our confession as the centre, but together with other confessions move as planets around the sun, the Christ.

Therefore my point is that speaking about systematic theology in ecumenical perspective is speaking about the essence and the character of systematic theology itself. It is not something extra that can be added or that can be left out if the teacher is not informed in ecumenics. It is not something that has to be stated explicitly about systematic theology. Teaching systematic theology in an ecumenical perspective is only possible if the teacher has not only some historical knowledge, but also some basic *convictions* about the character of systematic theology rooted in an actual confession of the church.

How much theology does a given church actually need? Many people have observed the shift in attention of the World Council from the classical theological differences and controversies between the churches, especially in Europe and the USA, to the reflection on the situation of third-world churches that must confess in their contexts. They consider it as a consequence of the fact that the hegemony of the European and American churches has been broken and that the European context no longer provides the universal frame for all theology, but has become one context among others.

I think we cannot decide beforehand how much theology a given situation needs. It is a healthy phenomenon that in a regular spring cleaning the ecumenical movement does away with all sorts of rubbish that has been packed in our theological attics and that we consequently can move a little more freely. This is especially important for the third-world churches that sometimes have lived too much under the impression that they had to digest the whole history of European churches and theology before they can arrive at something that belongs more authentically to themselves.

But it may well be that as they go on in their confrontation with their cultures and with the world of other faiths around them, similar needs for theology may become felt, as was the case in the development of theology in the undivided church for the first centuries, or that motives that were at stake in the Reformation come alive. The unmasking of heresy, which has been a strong agent in the development of systematic theology, is not a task that once and for all has been completed by the seven ecumenical councils of the undivided church. In the pursuit of the theme "gospel and culture" and the strong pleas we can hear for the adaptation to some cultures and the religious values of those cultures, the question of the identity of God as it is confessed by the Christian church can spring up in a new actuality and necessitate a good and thorough theological dialogue in which the experiences of the older Christian tradition that dealt with these issues might be useful and their answers regain a new actuality.

To teach systematic theology in an ecumenical perspective is to invite the students to a freedom of experience. It is launching out on a road where they can make experiences with the word of the gospel in a given situation in a new context, and by that experience enabling them to recognize experiences that the church has made before but of which the relevance was not yet sufficiently discovered.

Before I come to some methodological implications following what I have tried to develop, I would like to summarize the implications of my departure from the concept of confession. I have chosen it deliberately because I think that by its basic structure it can be recognized by all confessions as the basis of doctrinal development. It can also help to overcome the ambiguities arising out of the different meanings and expectations that are connected with the word "ecumenical". Without going into too much refinement, globally we can say that the word is used as referring to the "whole church" and to the "whole world", and sometimes people in using it suggest that we should choose between the two options: either for the whole church or for the whole world.

If however we begin our reflection on systematic theology in an ecumenical perspective, by focusing on the challenge to confess our *faith*, on *confession*, we cannot allow that alternative. If we confess the Lordship of Christ over the world, it is that which unites the church and unites it to the world. Confession is through the church for the whole world. It organically relates ecumenics to missiology. It shows that the alternative that is developed between the so-called "classical" and the so-called "contextual" theologies is false. "Classical" theologies were not abstract products but challenges to respond in situations and confess. "Contextual" theologies are not just the projections of experience but challenges to make audible the word of God in a given situation. This word does not arise out of the situation. It has to be heard and discovered in the gospel in the face of a situation. And when it has been heard, it has to be recognized by the rest of the church, also by that part of the church that does not live in such a situation.

In a confession a church speaks on behalf of the particular church to the whole church. If the churches have gone the way of critical self-investigation (that is to say critical in relation to our common tendency to defend our interests), then those who confess should have the courage not to speak for one confession only but require *ecumenical recognition* for their confession. The old church knew more about the differences in the situations and formulations of confessions than we seem to realize. But they knew also about the invitation to assemble, to share what we have confessed with those who live in other parts of the church and have confessed differently. In the periods when there were no councils, the bishops used to share with one another their formulation of the faith, their confessions, and ask for reception by the others. The consciousness of the existing and necessary differences in the expression of faith, according to the different contexts of the churches, was organically linked with the need and obligation that was felt to *share* these confessions. To come to one common expression of the apostolic faith (cf. the new project that has been taken up by Faith and Order) involves the sharing of our different expressions and, if necessary, the mutual questioning of these.

Methodological implications

Finally I would like to draw some methodological implications for teaching systematical theology in an ecumenical perspective.

1. From the parallel structures of "assembling" as the basic movement of the church and "putting things together" as the basic movement of systematic theology, it follows that teaching systematic theology in an ecumenical perspective should start by understanding itself as responsible for the unity among the different specializations in theology that have been developed by the need of division of labour but now tend to live a separate scientific life. It is a special responsibility of systematic theology to bring the analytic contributions of the separate disciplines of theology into one coherent perspective.

The first and main ecumenical perspective is that of the Christian *church*. This means that what has to be brought together in teaching systematic theology is primarily the organic relation between the foundation of the church in the gospel, its development through history (that is also the history of separations) to its actual proclamation in today's world. In terms of disciplines: the organic relation between exegesis (of Old and New Testament), history of the church and of the Christian doctrine and practical theology.

You may notice that I have deliberately left out two disciplines that sometimes are taught in theological faculties, philosophy and philosophical theology on the one hand, and the science or history of religions on the other. Both disciplines could argue that it is they that bring about the universalistic ecumenical atmosphere in theology. What could unite us more than a general, universalistic concept of human existence in the world, as it is developed in philosophy? Or what could liberate us more from our limited parochial Christian position than the vast world of religions? Teaching systematic theology in an ecumenical perspective, however, though directed to the outsider as far as our confession or group is concerned, very definitely considers those outsiders as *insiders* as far as the whole Christian church is concerned. Whatever one may believe about the use and the function of philosophical theology for apologetics, it has no place here. It would not take the ecumenical partner seriously as a Christian who shares the same basic presuppositions of a Christian, if at the same time we would try to find unity with him or her on a more general philosophical basis.

The general tendency of systematic theology that claims to be ecumenical is to begin with a philosophical analysis of the human situation, especially of creation. This is particularly so when the main partner in dialogue is Roman Catholic theology. Recent works like the new Dutch catechism, Hans Küng's *Christ-sein* (On Being a Christian), Karl Rahner's *Grundkurs des Glaubens* (Fundamental Course of Faith) and Neues Glaubensbuch (edited by Johannes Feiner and Lukas Vischer) start with a large section on "Die Frage nach Gott" (the question of God). The universalist perspective of the Christian faith however does not lie in the beginning, but in the end. Not in creation, but in eschatology.

The same holds true in regard to a possible inclusion of the other religions in the teaching of systematics in ecumenical perspective. Apart from the fact that even among scholars of religion there is no agreement over a general concept of religion, we would not take our ecumenical partners seriously as Christians if we began by involving them in a discussion of other religions. Whether interfaith dialogue has a place in systematic theology should only be discussed *after* and not before ecumenical theology.

2. Teaching systematic theology in ecumenical perspective therefore should start on the basis of scripture and its scientific and open exegesis. It is the common belief of all Christian traditions that the gospel that united us is found in scripture. This choice is not because "scripture" is the end of all dogmatic controversies, as was believed in the past. Scripture itself contains a plurality of theological positions. But the plurality of theological positions was brought into a perspective of unity by the creation of the canon of the Bible through which the church perceives unity in the plurality, the convergence of all confessions around the central confession of Jesus as Lord.

The plurality of "theologies" that was detected in scripture in the first phase of the ecumenical movement was considered to be a threat to its unifying principle, before it could be integrated as a liberating principle. At the world conference of faith and order in 1963 in Montreal, Ernst Käsemann asked whether the biblical canon did not rather produce the plurality of confessions than the unity of the church.[11] At first his contribution brought confusion for those who believed that even when the churches have conflicts, and live in disunity, they can be healed by returning to the unity of scripture. But afterwards it was felt that the perspective of a plurality instead of the romantic concept of unity at the beginning can help ecumenical work more than hinder it. The plurality of perspectives in which in the New Testament the gospel becomes visible has favoured the quest for the unity and the development of theology. We could consider the three main basic structures that have been developed in the plurality of beginnings in the old church, canon, dogma and ministry, as necessary elements of development on the road from diversity to unity. It is a movement that has to be redone in theology again and again, not only under the conditions of the old church or of the Reformation but in the situation of our time and culture as well.

A word about the role of the so-called biblical theology in the exercise of teaching systematics in ecumenical perspective. From what has been said before, it might be concluded that in our concept which starts with exegesis, biblical theology might play a key role in the process of transition of exegesis to systematics. It would then accord with the important role biblical theology has played for a long time in the ecumenical movement and that has led to the favouring of such half-exegetical, half-systematical concepts as "history of salvation".[12] But there is a danger too in developing a separate biblical theology between exegesis and systematic theology. Exegesis is an open procedure, done in the expectation that through a penetration into the word of scripture, the gospel shall become clear for today. In the same way, however, as dogmatics may not be confounded with a rounded-off systematic theology, a biblical theology may not be designed as a plurality of rounded-off biblical witnesses that have spoken differently to their respective situations. That would be a fixation and a systematizing of an open process of exegesis that would be no less ideological in character than the fixation of that process in such enterprises as materialistic or feminist exegesis. The orientation of the biblical testimony towards a reactualization of the proclamation of the gospel should not be replaced by the juxtaposition of a plurality of theologies. The idea of the canon is the translation of the intuition of the early church that plurality is not the last word, but that the unity that is audible in this plurality should remain also for us a constant point of orientation.

3. The next step in the organizing of unity in theology that is the special responsibility of the teacher of ecumenics is the integration of church history and the

history of doctrine under the viewpoint of the disintegration of the Christian church. The history of the church is also the history of how the divisions and separations of the Christian church came into being. All available facts and factors should be recognized. The systematic theologian is not less interested in the so-called "non-theological" factors than in the so-called "theological" factors; it has long been recognized that the former are often more relevant theologically than the history of ideas treated in the history of doctrine. Neither a materialistic nor an idealistic view of church history should prejudice the open observation of all relevant factors. Of course the study of church history under the perspective of studying the origins of church divisions is a selective option, as every study of history is conditioned by the questions we pose; but as this selective option it is the background for the deliberate systematic attempt to bring the separated churches together.

But not only the negative aspects of the separations between the existing churches will come to light in the study of church history; it is also the study of the expansion and establishing the church in new areas that created new partner-churches in the ecumenical dialogue, partners who can help the older churches that labour under the bad effects of their confessionalism, in understanding afresh the original sense of what "confession" is.

4. It might seem that all that was said before about the integration of the totality of theology as the task for the teacher of systematic theology would not leave him any special task, and that I was attempting to put the whole load of the ecumenical perspective on the shoulders of other colleagues. That however is not the case. Through the enlarged consciousness of the plurality of theologies and the divisions of churches a special scientific operation is needed to encounter the existing divisions and make visible and conscious the experience of a new growing unity between the churches.

This special scientific operation should make use of all the tools that actual systematic theology has at its disposal. The older method of comparative dogmatics is no longer sufficient. As it is built upon the assumption of the homogeneity of the language and the concepts that are compared, it does not see that sometimes a translation from one structure of anthropological and historical concepts into another is necessary in order to discover all the possibilities of convergence that were not discovered before, or to discover the real differences that might have lain hidden under an outward convergence in words. Unity in doctrine is not necessarily identical with unity in the formulation of the doctrine. Not only a *biblical* hermeneutics is necessary, but also a *dogmatic hermeneutics* and a hermeneutics to compare different *church structures* expressed in *church law*. Edmund Schlink, the German pioneer of ecumenical systematic theology, in his magnum opus *Ökumenische Dogmatik* that appeared shortly before his death two years ago, has brought in in a very convincing way this new method of comparing doctrine. [13]

He has pointed out also that systematic theology in ecumenical perspective should not limit itself to the study of putting together and distinguishing the existing doctrinal expression of the church. It should also reckon with the possibility of such dogmatic statements that have not yet been realized in the history of dogma and church. Schlink seriously reckons with this possibility of new dogmatic statements that will arise out of the encounter of the gospel with the spiritual world especially of Asia.

66

This brings us to our final remarks about the role and the responsibility of the systematic theologian as he or she works in ecumenical perspective. As the teacher of dogmatics during a long time was considered to be the *defensor fidei*, in the sense of the official ideologue of one's church or group, one should now be permitted to be the pioneer on paths that hitherto have remained unexplored. In the prolongation of the perspective that is already present in any dogmatic work, challenged through one's constant task to put things together, one always discovers more things that have to be put together than one had assumed before. One is challenged to put these new things together as well, not in a closed system, a bastion of "truths" that has to be defended, but in an *open* system.

Teaching systematic theology in ecumenical perspective is inviting students into this open field, starting from scripture, and letting the totality of it work on them in its force and clarity. The reformers confessed — over against the Roman Catholic position that scripture can function as the basis of theology only if it is in the last resort explained by the authority of the magisterium of the church — the doctrine of the *perspicuitas sacrae scripturae*, the clarity and the transparence of holy scripture. And it may be the special ecumenical vocation of the Reformation (that has not yet been fully realized) to show in an exemplary, ecumenical way that scripture is sufficiently transparent to bring about unity in theology, sufficiently rich to justify a variety of accents, and sufficiently unexplored yet to yield surprises.

In going into those new and unexpected dimensions, however, we do not move away from what we and the church have confessed before in our confessions, but on the contrary, more deeply into it. As it is expressed in an unsurpassable way in Ephesians 3:18: "With deep roots and firm foundations, may you be strong to grasp, with all God's people, what is the breadth and the length and height and depth of the love of Christ, and to know it, though it is beyond knowledge. So may you attain to fullness of being, the fullness of God himself."

Here it is clearly stated that the last perspective of ecumenical theology is not the unity of the church, nor the unity of the world, but the Triune Being of God. The communion with all the others that we seek is a quality of God. God is communion, in the glory of God's life as Father, Son and Holy Ghost, and as such God communicates himself to us in Jesus Christ. For God is not the prisoner of God's own identity, but the overflowing source of communion. "The cistern contains, the fountain overflows" (William Blake): the cistern has its circumscribed identity, but the fountain has its identity in that it overflows.

To do or teach systematic theology in an ecumenical perspective, to discover the identity of the Christian faith, is to be ready to be surprised by the ever new dimensions of the love of God.

NOTES

[1] K.H. Miskotte, "De moderne dogmaticus als dilettant en dirigent", in *Geloof en Kennis*, Haarlem, 1966, pp.307-322. German translation: "Der moderne Dogmatiker als Dilettant und Dirigent", in *Ev. Theol.*, 20, 1960.
[2] K.L. Schmidt, art. "ekklesia", in *Th. W.N.T.*, III, 505.
[3] Cf. G. Sauter, art. Dialogik II, in *Theologische Realenzyklopädie*, Vol. 8, pp.703-705

[4] *Die Ökumenische Utopie, oder: Was bewegt die ökumenische Bewegung?*, Stuttgart, 1972 (English: *And Yet It Moves*).

[5] IV, 3, 1, p.37.

[6] Cf. *The Ecumenical Review*, Vol. 37, No. 2, April 1985, "The WCC Basis".

[7] Decree on Ecumenism of Vatican Council II, nr. 11. Cf. J.C. Hampe, *Die Autorität der Freiheit*, II, pp.619-624.

[8] J. Feiner and L. Vischer eds, *Neues Glaubensbuch*, Zurich, 1973, p.16

[9] Cf. W.A. Visser 't Hooft, "Karl Barth und die ökumenische Bewegung", in *Ev. Theol.*, January/February 1980, p.6.

[10] Preface by H. Fries to *Ökumenische Dogmatik*, Edmund Schlink, Göttingen, 1984, XVII.

[11] Ernst Käsemann, "Einheit und Vielfalt in der neutestamentlichen Lehre von der Kirche", in *Exegetische Versuche und Besinnungen*, II, pp.262-267. Cf. "Begründet der neutestamentliche Kanon die Einheit der Kirche?", in *Exegetische Versuche und Besinnungen*, I, pp.214-223

[12] Cf. E. Lessing "Die Bedeutung der Heilsgeschichte in der ökumenischen Diskussion", in *Ev. Theol.*, May/June 1984

[13] *Ökumenische Dogmatik* (see note 10). For the three kinds of hermeneutics, see especially: Chap. XXI, A.3. Grundlinien einer biblischen Hermeneutik (pp.637-646), Chap. XXI, B.3. Grundlinien einer dogmatischen Hermeneutik (pp.655-660), Chap. XXI, C.3. Zur kirchenrechtlichen Hermeneutik (pp.669-673).

7. The God-talk of the Oppressed: an Asian Contribution

David Kwang-sun Suh

Towards ideological independence

I have been teaching systematic theology at both undergraduate and graduate departments of Christian studies in the faculty of liberal arts of a traditional mission school in Korea. Like most theological seminaries and academic departments of theology, we organized our four-year undergraduate curriculum with core courses on the Bible, church history, systematic theology, ethics, preaching, religious education, worship, etc. Most of the teachers in these institutions are recognized by Western institutions of theological education as academically qualified teachers and research-ers, trained in one or more Western languages besides their own mother tongue. We theological teachers mostly follow and imitate what our Western teachers were doing when we were students, sometimes with feelings of inadequacy and frustration because of the lack of library resources and the students' limited language ability to read the great Western theological authors. So we become involved in the develop-ment of theological textbooks, which are mostly translations of the famous "classical" books we became familiar with when we were studying theology in the West. Teaching theology in our part of the world is thus mostly translation work: it is to translate the Western authors into our native language, and it is also to translate the culture-laden Western Christian theological concepts into our own language to make them sensible and meaningful.

Problems arise, however, when the Western Christian theological concepts and dogmas do not make sense at all in our native language. The traditional way of solving this problem was to memorize the whole body of Christian dogma, letter by letter, without making any connection with the social and historical context from which these concepts and dogmas had come. Our Western missionary theological teachers handed down to us native converts a package of ready-made theological concepts and dogmas, and we swallowed them as an important part of believing in the new religion and of following the way of Jesus Christ. Our missionary theological mentors were inadequate in translating the difficult theological concepts into the strange language; they had only limited skill in the native tongue and they were not trained theological teachers. There had been little theological development in the churches in Asia, where the dominant theological ideology was fundamental-ism, until the time when the colonized countries gained political independence from Western imperialism in the 1940s.

During the last forty years, in spite of political independence, or the struggle for it, Christian theology in formerly colonized countries — like most other academic fields of study in the universities in these countries — has not gained ideological independence. The Korean theologians could speak Korean better than the American missionaries when they taught theology and preached in the churches. But the language problem still remained: they had to translate the Western concepts and Christian dogmas from English or German into Korean, but such language skill was as limited as that of the missionary teachers when they spoke Korean.

Since I came back to Korea from the United States in the late sixties, I have enthusiastically introduced to my students the theologies of Tillich, Bultmann, Bonhoeffer, Moltmann and Harvey Cox, because I was excited about them when I was studying in American theological schools. But I only created confusion and frustration among my students. Tillich's "ground of being" is beyond the philosophical imagination of our students. Bultmann's demythologization is not only tongue-twisting; it shocked their fundamentalist, anti-hermeneutic understanding of the Bible. In the theological climate of Korea, where Karl Barth's thinking is condemned as dangerous liberal theology, an introduction of the whole theological enterprise of the last two centuries in the West is itself a new way of teaching/doing/learning theology.

What is new about introducing contemporary Western theologians? It is new because these names are unheard-of, either because of theological ignorance or because of ecclesial prohibition. But it is also new because these theologians themselves introduced new ways of doing theology in the Western society. Paul Tillich took culture seriously, even though the culture he spoke of was high-brow Western bourgeois culture. He made me talk positively about our Asian religions and traditional culture and about the existential situation from which theological questions arise. Bultmann opened up a wide horizon to my students, enabling them to read the Bible from an entirely different perspective, even going beyond his existential interpretation of the kerygma. The reading of Bonhoeffer's prison letters in Korean translation has made our students think about the political history of Korean Christians, which is filled with martyrs standing up against the ideological idols of the dominant powers. While Harvey Cox introduced the secular world of the West to our students, they incorporated him into their experience of revolutionary struggles for the building of a new nation. Moltmann's theological writings stimulated our political imagination and enabled us to interpret our theological politics.

What is new in these theologians' doing of theology was that they took their world seriously: Bonhoeffer took Nazi Germany seriously; Cox took his secular American society seriously; and Moltmann took the political world of the West seriously. I do not know whether these theologians thought of themselves as doing and teaching theology from the ecumenical perspective, but I think when we take the real, concrete, political and social world seriously in doing theology, it is the ecumenical way of doing theology.

The whole question of theological legitimacy used to be a question of the academic standard set by the Western theological schools and the denominational authorities. But in the new way of doing theology, I have discovered that theological legitimacy depends on its relation to the world. The new way of doing theology is theologically responsible to the world: it is doing theology *from* the world, *for* the world and *in* the world. This is, as I learned in my situation, the responsible ecumenical way of doing theology.

Starting from our own world

Once we realize that our Western contemporary theologians are taking this world seriously in their doing of theology, we do not have to stay with their theological writings alone, thinking about their theological struggles in their Western context. Now we can turn to our own context, to our own world. That is to say, we start our theologizing anew; we do not start from the Western theological package, but from our own world of politics, economics, traditional religions, and our native cultures. As we interpret what Western Christian thinkers are saying in their own context, we begin interpreting the Bible and Christian traditions from our own perspective of our own world. When we take our world seriously and try to respond to it, the problem of hermeneutical suspicion comes up. We cannot simply use the entire Western ideological framework of Christian theology in our reading of the Bible and in our mission of word and action. We have to critically question the dominant ideology of Western Christian theologies in our doing/teaching/learning, in our experience of the contemporary political world.

Until I was forced to confront the powerful military dictatorship of the 1970s in Korea, which was, to me, the most concrete and real world of politics, I did teach systematic theology in the comfortable world of Western philosophy and liberal ideologies, interpreting Western political and philosophical theologies. But when I took the risk of losing my respectable position as university professor, by signing petitions and political statements for the Christian and secular student democratic human rights movement, I was forced to take my political world seriously in my actual doing and teaching of theology. I had to learn how to articulate my theology and biblical understanding as I drafted political statements and declarations for the humanization of politics and for economic justice for the workers and disinherited farmers in the rapidly and forcibly industrializing society of Korea. Our doing theology in such a political situation is critical and confrontational: we have to be critical of the dominant ideology in both politics and in the churches; we have to confront the most powerful ideological superstructure of the dominant political system. We also have to discover a new way of reading the Bible on the basis of our political struggles, and to construct an eschatological vision of the kingdom of God which is operative in our history.

Our job of doing and teaching theology has not been limited to the confines of classrooms, church podiums, and lecture halls. We have had to go out into the world: holding ecumenical conferences, open forums and theological debates, drafting political statements, holding seminars with labour union workers and farmers' movement members. Sometimes we have been taken into the police torture chambers for an investigation of our theological lectures and political statements. Some of us have had to end up in prison. And when we come back again into the classrooms to teach Augustine, Barth, Bonhoeffer, Moltmann, Jim Cone and Gutierrez, we talk about them from the perspective of the world as we have experienced it. Our theological language can no longer be the *ghetto* language of the comfortable academia of dignity and authority. It should become the humble language of the world, full of anger, ambiguity, and frustration against the evil in the world. Thus our God-talk becomes alive, like the action of God in the world. And our God-talk is inevitably iconoclastic and exorcistic. Our teaching of systematic theology has to become a systematic destruction of the ideological idols of Christian religion. And our doing of theology is the exorcising act of casting out the political demons in the world. Identifying and naming the idols and devils in the Christian churches in our cultures is the first task of teaching theology in an ecumenical way. This is the reason why, in the process of teaching systematic theology, we have to call on the help of those who have been doing "philosophical theology" in a new way. The new way is not to "philosophize" theology but to make a connection between faith and ideology. The new way of doing theology is not only just to understand what theology is, but to change it, and with it to change the world.

The doing of theology in an ecumenical way in the traditionally non-Christian world of Asia includes an extra task. The non-Christian world is based on a religious-cultural-ideological superstructure which is totally ignorant of and alien to the Christian ideological superstructure of the Western world. The task of doing theology in a non-Christian world goes far beyond doing translating work. We must take the language of the non-Christian world seriously as we undertake the hermeneutical task. We should be liberated from the illusion that the theologians' task is to speak about the Christian God in the heathen world. The language and culture of the heathen world must interpret the gospel, as the heathen world of the Greeks and Romans took up the hermeneutical task of understanding the Christian gospel. Thus, our task of doing theology in this "heathen" world has to become *creative*. Going beyond learning and teaching Western "heathen" cultures and religious ideologies, we have found ourselves learning and teaching Asian cultures and religions in order to see how this alien Christian gospel took such deep root in the superstructure of the Eastern ideologies. Our task of doing theology in the Eastern "heathen" world has to be creative as we try to interpret the gospel in the language and culture from which we have come. Like American black theologians and feminist theologians, we can no longer be consumers of Western theological products — feeling and thinking as if we have become Western persons. We have to create our own way of speaking about God from our deep and rich resources of traditional culture and Asian religions. As we took our traditional culture and religion seriously, we have come to realize that our tradition is not something inferior or incomplete, but is complete and sufficient as part of God's creation.

The need to reshape curriculum

Therefore, the whole theological curriculum has to be reshaped and reorganized when you take your own world seriously. Those of us who do and teach theology in this part of the world cannot, as in the past, organize our own theological teaching schedules as our Western theological teachers did. We cannot spend all of our time reading Augustine, Aquinas, Calvin, Luther, Kant, Hegel, Schleiermacher, Feuerbach, Barth, Bultmann and Tillich, and interpreting them to our young students who are only awed by our incomprehensible and irrelevant language of theology in the context of their contemporary struggle for living. The bringing of our world into the scene of doing theology cannot be a spare-time or extra-curricular effort. So to speak, we cannot only consume the Western-made Christian theological "care"[1] package.

When we take our world seriously, we have to take seriously those contemporary theologians who took their world seriously. And when we find ourselves doing the dangerous and risky work of idol-breaking and exorcising, we identify ourselves in solidarity with those ecumenical theologians who have been working for the liberation of theology and for the liberative task of theology. We bring together in our task of doing theology, Latin American liberation theology, feminist Christian theology, American black theology, and liberational political theology in the Western world. And we learn from them how they have brought together their experience in transforming their hermeneutical framework, how they have related their faith to ideology, how they have broken their own religious and ideological idols, and how they have taken the suffering people's stories seriously. To use Prof. Geense's language, finally, we learn from them how they *confessed* their faith in their particular situation.

Furthermore, when we take the task of theology as liberative and liberating, we bring our own world into our doing of theology. In our doing of theology we have to understand the basic structural character of our contemporary political-economic world, in order to understand and name the physical, mental and spiritual suffering of the people. We have to understand the dominant ideological superstructure of oppression, in order to understand the suffering of God and what God is doing in this world with the people.

In order to understand our Christian religion, we have to examine our hermeneutical framework, our traditional cultural and religious framework from and through which we interpret and understand the Christian gospel. Non-Christian religions are not only the ideological superstructure of our world, but they are also rich resources from which we can reshape our ideology in relation to our faith. We must bring non-Christian religions into our task of doing theology, as our theological forerunners have insisted on bringing non-Christian worldviews and myths into their task of doing theology in their world. As they were creative in their doing of theology, we can and ought to be creative in our doing of theology in our world.

As we take our world seriously, we must take the people who are suffering and struggling for liberation seriously. The stories of our suffering people in our particular world have to be brought into our task of doing theology. And those stories ought to be told as vividly and as passionately as we can. If we ignore and forget the socio-biography of the people, we might fall into the serious mistake of ignoring and forgetting the spoken socio-biography of the people of Israel, and the voice with which God has spoken to us. We have to re-read our own political history not just as the history of domination of the powerful, but as the history of the suffering and liberation of the people of God.

The ultimate task of doing systematic theology is to hear and articulate the word of God and to confess our faith in Jesus Christ; then our experiences, theological, political, cultural and socio-biographical, should be brought together to make our theology and confession meaningful and powerful, to change the world and liberate our theology. Thus, our doing/teaching/learning of systematic theology is a constant writing and rewriting of our confession of faith, and that confession is written not only in the secluded place of the altar or lecture hall, but also in open, public places where our act of confession can be seen and heard by the oppressors and exploiters.

Doing systematic theology in an ecumenical way is doing theology in the world. And teaching systematic theology in an ecumenical perspective is doing it from the perspective of the world and of the suffering and oppressed people of God. Therefore, doing theology becomes dangerous and risky; it means taking up the costly discipleship which follows the cross of Jesus Christ himself. Doing theology in an ecumenical way demands commitment to the liberation of theology and of the oppressed people of God.

NOTE

[1] CARE stands for Cooperative for American Remittance to Europe. But during the Korean war (1950–53) "CARE" package was sent to Korean war refugees for food and clothing.

8. Ecumenics and Interfaith Dialogue

An Interfaith Methodology

Mary Hall

The word "adventure" is defined in the dictionary as a "daring enterprise", an "unexpected incident". If we are lucky we encounter many of them in our lives; some we have the courage to choose, some we avoid, and some we have thrust upon us. One of the latter in my case was acceding to the request of the Catholic Bishops' Conference of England and Wales in 1978 to initiate a research project in dialogue between people of different religions in Birmingham.

The question was how to establish a multifaith research project in Birmingham with its 12 percent proportion of ethnic minorities, where Christian communities have little to do with each other and certainly no contact with neighbouring Jews, Hindus, Muslims, Sikhs and Buddhists. Eight years as an education adviser in Pakistan had taught me that getting groups together for discussion of beliefs can lead to individual friendships based on tolerance and respect, but it very often leads also to arguments and intellectual discussion that become sterile and in no way promote real dialogue.

The vision I had of Birmingham was that of a jigsaw of various religions, each piece representing the truth of that particular tradition. From experience I knew it would be necessary for the groups to speak for themselves rather than participate in a survey or answer a relevant questionnaire. So I began a search for groups of 8 to 12 people willing to attempt constructive interaction. It took many months, during which I met various Christian groups "busy about many things", bazaars, concerts, bring-and-buys, but reluctant to get involved in any kind of self-analysis of belief and practice for sharing with others.

I also met many non-Christian groups who had been subjected to countless surveys of one kind or another and who were slow to believe they would be allowed to speak for themselves. Many of them were convinced there was some ulterior motive other than growth in understanding behind the request. Finally, I succeeded in getting several groups together who fulfilled the research requirements of residence in Birmingham and a religious faith central to their way of life. It was established from the beginning that respect for each group's beliefs was as important as emphasizing the differences.

When the groups met for the first time the phrase was used that "fences were necessary for living". Someone suggested that perhaps the research would enable gates to be made rather than the breaking down of fences. A West Indian Pentecostal pastor replied that from where he sat there was an enormous fence and his concern was: could he keep his fence intact while participating in the research? To which a Buddhist present rejoined: "To you this may seem important but to us as Buddhists there are no essential differences between people, only the appearance of difference. We have no fences." The dialogue had begun. Ultimately, 14 groups of 8 to 12 people — in all, 156 — agreed to participate in a three-year project. The groups were Anglican, Bethel Apostolic Pentecostal, Church of Christ, German Evangelical Lutheran, Hindu, Mahayana Buddhist, Methodist, Orthodox Jew, Progressive Jew, Roman Catholic, Shiloh Pentecostal, Sikh, Theravadan Buddhist, United Reformed.

At the outset, the members were complete strangers to each other. It was the first time they had met or sat in the same room together. When a representative steering committee was set up, members at first talked only to their own representatives. Historical tensions showed: if Muslims spoke the Hindus remained silent, explanations by Jews brought little response from Christians, and so on. The groups met separately to discuss various agreed themes, and compiled reports which were circulated to all the other groups.

During the preparation of these the group leaders visited me regularly, and one morning a Jewish neighbour asked me, very seriously and politely, what was the reason for the frequent visits of coloured gentlemen with briefcases to my flat! After several meetings with all those involved, where we analyzed the reports and shared our deepest convictions, prejudices and misunderstandings came out into the open, and trust and openness began to build.

A year and a half into the research it was agreed to work in multifaith groups, and if possible, for extended periods of time. When and where was the difficulty? To find a day suitable for all was not easy. Fridays didn't suit the Muslims, Saturdays the Jews, Sundays the Christians, especially the Pentecostals who spend most of the day in church. Finally a period from mid-day to four o'clock on Sundays every six weeks was agreed; the local Methodist church hall was the venue, with a vegetarian meal to avoid complications.

For a further 18 months we discussed the problems of citizenship faced by all. I remember one role-play session in particular — a couple meeting the resident housing committee of a block of flats. The couple presenting their case was an articulate Sikh and his role-play wife — a very articulate Christian who had learnt from the research experience to remain silent during the interview — while a committee of Muslims, Hindus, Buddhists and Jews voiced their objections to accepting further Asians into the building. Through such sessions the groups began to affirm the unique contribution they made to the same social, economic and political reality. They also discovered aspects of their own beliefs and practices which needed further study, and more importantly they affirmed their responsibility to work together as citizens in an increasingly irreligious society. As we came towards the end of the three-year project people commented that they had learnt not only about other faiths, but so much more about their own beliefs and practices by having to explain them to others. Many felt a sense of loss at the thought that mutual cooperation and learning was coming to an end. As one Muslim phrased it: "We have learned to understand and trust one another; is it not possible to continue doing so?"

From many such comments emerged the idea of a multifaith resource unit, an organization of groups respecting the integrity of their different beliefs, but ready to

learn from each other. They defined themselves as an association of people who attempt to:
— provide a space and opportunity for people from different religious backgrounds and cultures to work at understanding each other's beliefs, theology and traditions, in relation to what they share together;
— innovate new types of religious studies blending the insights and experiences of basic communities of different faiths with the scholarship of traditional religious studies;
— promote carefully selected and creative joint religious, social and economic action programmes and activities, and provide concerned support for each other in times of stress and need.

During the research project we learnt the significance of faith as a central factor in the culture of different groups. We learnt the value of clarifying and understanding by taking time to examine our religious beliefs and practices. We learnt to appreciate the space given in which to examine what we and others, with our varying beliefs and practices stood for, and how to mutually interact with integrity. We learnt the value of providing time and opportunity so that groups could trust each other enough to learn from each other.

Since the unit was established five years ago we have continued to learn many new values and to rediscover others that had been lost or submerged, for example, the true value of community, the meaning of honest sharing, sensitivity to others, the virtue of hospitality and the importance of meditation and prayer to enable us to live with the tension between the physical, cultural and spiritual aspects of our lives.

A recent paper by Cardinal Francis A. Arinze, president of the Secretariat for Non-Christians, notes that:

> Formation to inter-religious dialogue is to be regarded as an essential part of Christian catechesis. This means that seminaries should give the subject a good place in their curriculum. The Christians in each country have to pay special attention to the non-Christian religions in their midst. Christians who oppose dialogue, or who suspect it or regard it as unnecessary, are to be helped to come out of their entrenched positions.
>
> There are some countries, in Europe for example, where until about forty years ago most of the people were Christians (even if many were not practising), but where there are now significant numbers of immigrant workers of non-Christian religions. These latter have rightly brought with them their religions. They have, or need to have, their places of worship. They are spreading their faith to others. There are marriages between them and Christians.

The church in such countries is now bound to seek ways to form its Christians stronger in the faith, taking into account the other religions in their midst. If this is not done, Christians will not be able to meet the situation adequately; they will not be able to present Christianity well to their neighbours of other faiths; some of them will become weak in their faith or begin to doubt, and some of them will abandon Christianity altogether and go over to other religions. Furthermore, it is essential that we cooperate ecumenically in interfaith work.

In any situation, the authentic proclamation of the gospel is a witness by word, by the silent witness of action, or by the even more silent presence of a gospel life lived faithfully among others. At the same time it is a listening to life, discovering the presence of God's word and Spirit among a people, a presence which has preceded the missionary. In this way the light of the gospel can continually illuminate the signs of the times to manifest the language which is to be used by the one who proclaims the gospel here and now.[1]

The goal of proclamation can therefore be understood according to two models, different but complementary:

a) *Extending the visible communion of the church:* Proclamation here has a "centripetal" purpose, leading people directly into the church, which in this way becomes a visible communion, implanted within a people in a way that it is capable of growing into a full institutional reality.

b) *Recognizing and furthering the values of the kingdom:* Proclamation in this model has a "centrifugal" purpose, allowing the power of the gospel to move out and encounter humanity in its struggles and diversity. It entails in the one who proclaims a readiness to seek the Christ he or she announces. This kind of proclamation of the gospel is fruitful when it promotes and furthers the values of the kingdom within a culture and denounces and inhibits what is not of the kingdom of God.

Jesus spoke of the kingdom being near at hand, among us, yet-to-be but here already. He told people they could, or could not, enter it, but never said they were in it. Only one man was said to be "not far from it". The kingdom was in history, yet always more than expected. It was always appreciated as gift — as grace — but it was never magic. It demanded all the preparation and pre-disposition that gift-receiving does demand.

Like all love affairs, the kingdom was enigmatic, better talked of in stories and celebration than in books and theses. And like all love affairs it was recognized only by those who knew it by experience. You could know it but not know about it.

I have come to think that the main thrust of all Jesus' preaching was to persuade people to accept this antecedent reality of God's presence and creativity. It is the love of God in people's lives, God's antecedent kingdom, which urges us. It is not the building of something on God's behalf, this spectator-God waiting for us to do great things in God's name.

"How I envy you British," said an East German pastor attending one of the unit's programmes. "You only have to step over your doorstep into the street and you can meet people who represent all the great challenges to the Christian faith today — Muslims, Hindus, Sikhs, Jews, atheists, humanists, people of every possible background and outlook. What a wonderful chance to grow into the riches that God has stored for us ready in his kingdom. At home we can talk only to Communists!"

NOTE

[1] *Gaudium et Spes*, 4.

9. Dialogue with People of Other Faiths and Ecumenical Theology

J. Paul Rajashekar

Christian ecumenism, as we have come to understand it in the course of this century, has been primarily concerned with intra-ecclesial unity. In the face of the plurality of theological positions and diversity of cultural expressions, it has been an ongoing pilgrimage on the part of churches in search of unity or a collective sense of identity without stifling diversity. With every progress made in visible expressions of unity or consensus in theological self-understanding, our horizons have gradually expanded. As this journey continues, the concerns of Christian ecumenical theology will be increasingly widened to include extra-ecclesial issues which impinge upon our evolving self-understanding and theological task.

Christian relations with people of other faiths is one such issue that has come into prominence in Christian experience in recent decades and demands our attention. This brief contribution is an attempt to articulate the significance of that demand for our ecumenical theology.

Religions and ecumenical theology

It may be recalled that at the World Missionary Conference in Edinburgh (1910), the most important milestone of the ecumenical movement, the struggle for Christian unity was primarily motivated by the larger concern of Christian mission in the world. It was of course still a period of Christian missionary expansion in continents inhabited by people who adhered to other religions. Thus the challenge posed by those other religions for Christian mission and Christian theological articulation could not be overlooked in early ecumenical discussions. This was evident in the subsequent missionary conferences held in Jerusalem (1928) and Tambaram (1938) where the relationship of Jesus Christ to non-Christian religions, cultures and other secularized contexts was the central topic of discussion. It was to be expected that this discussion would be pursued within the framework of a missionary understanding of the church, and under the influence of the theology of Karl Barth and Hendrik Kraemer the focus was clearly on the significance of the gospel for other religions and cultures.

The lively debate that had begun was unfortunately interrupted by the Second World War. But the subsequent post-colonial developments, especially the resurgence of ancient religions, the spread of new secular ideologies and a revived sense of nationalism in many contexts, offered a new framework for a missiological discussion on other religions. The new-found awareness of the responsibility of the churches in nation-building and social reform in Asian and African contexts promoted a search for a dialogical relationship with adherents of other faiths. Thus from the latter part of the 1950s onwards, Christian relations with people of other faiths emerged again as a priority concern in ecumenical discussions. It was only in 1968, however, that a special WCC programme on relations with other faiths was established. By then there were significant developments in Roman Catholic theological thinking as well, and Vatican II had already issued the "Declaration on the Relation of the Church to Non-Christian Religions."[1] Thus dialogue with other faiths became firmly established as an ongoing concern in the ecumenical movement.

Within the WCC family the adoption of "Guidelines on Dialogue" (1977, 1979) is a significant step forward. This brief document reflects the later developments in ecumenical thinking on Christian relations to other faiths and puts the emphasis on "dialogue in community". But it also alludes to certain theological issues that need to be further addressed. Some of these issues had already been hotly debated in Tambaram and afterwards. But the debate had remained inconclusive and in mentioning some of those theological issues the document aims at reviving that discussion. It is noteworthy, however, that the section is entitled "The Theological Significance of People of Other Faiths and Ideologies". This title is suggestive of a subtle shift in perspective. In the earlier ecumenical debate the focus was clearly on "the significance of the gospel" for other faiths and cultures and the discussion thus took place within the framework of a missiological debate. But the Christian experience in inter-religious dialogue and our broadened awareness of the faith and values of others in recent decades have had some impact on how we pose the question of our relations with people of other faiths. By seeking to explore the theological significance of other faiths for the Christian faith, the future discussion is bound to move to the centre of Christian ecumenical theology.

It is clear that Christian relations with people of other faiths has been a long-standing concern in the ecumenical movement, although primarily in one stream of ecumenical thinking (i.e. the former International Missionary Council). Given that long history of discussions, one would expect the theological concerns arising out of our encounter with other faiths to receive greater attention in ecumenical theology. But unfortunately what has emerged as "ecumenical theology" has yet to integrate those concerns into its structures of discussion. What has so far been commonly understood as "ecumenical theology" has by and large been preoccupied with the issue of intra-ecclesial unity. It is of course understandable that matters of Christian faith and order — which have divided the church for centuries — require special attention and sustained international Christian dialogue. It has indeed been a matter of priority for Christians that they learn to understand and affirm their faith collectively and this process will need to continue in the future.

But have we not reached a point in our ecumenical pilgrimage where ecumenical theology could now begin to broaden the scope and contents of its discussion? Can Christian self-identity be defined in isolation from vital theological issues and concerns that impinge on Christian existence in the world, such as the challenges of poverty and oppression, of justice and peace, of other faiths and ideologies? Is not our ecumenical theology likely to run the risk of becoming so introverted, ecclesio-centred and self-celebrating that its own ecumenical vision of seeking to reach the whole oikoumene is undermined? What is the relation of the church, which seeks to confess the one faith in Jesus, to the wider community of people? Can the self-definition of Christian community be deepened in a more inclusive way through our encounters with people of other living faiths?

Such questions pose a challenge to Christian ecumenical theology and urge it to move from its self-legitimating preoccupations towards a total vision of ecumenism: the unity of the church and the unity of humankind. They may help redeem oikoumene from its ethnocentric connotations and help ecumenical theology to regain a true awareness that "the oikoumene is the whole inhabited earth and not just the Christian part of it".

The preceding observations need not necessarily undermine the distinction that is often made between ecumenism in the narrow sense of the unity of Christians and the wider ecumenism involving the unity and renewal of humankind. These two aspects are not mutually exclusive although in point of fact Christian ecumenical discussion tends to treat them separately. It is the task of Christian ecumenical theology to strive to bring them into mutual interaction, both dialogically and dialectically. Any exclusive emphasis on one or the other would only undermine the integrity of a truly ecumenical theology. In other words, an ecumenical theology which focuses exclusively on the search for Christian unity may well turn out to be narcissistic; on the other hand it may become self-destructive if it focuses exclusively on a wider, secular ecumenism with no place for the church. It is important therefore that a sound ecumenical theology be both introspective and truly open to the world.

Towards a dialogical theology

In a real sense all theological articulations are engaged in or products of dialogue or conversation. This has been true throughout the history of Christian theology and is especially true in the case of twentieth century theology. In the narrower sense, ecumenical theology is a product of a sustained bilateral and multilateral dialogue between various Christian confessional families which have taken place in many ecumenical conferences. These intra-Christian dialogues were indeed grounded in some shared presuppositions, although divergently articulated among the various theological traditions. Interconfessional dialogues were basically an attempt to clarify those theological assumptions which had given rise to a plurality of theological positions within Christianity, in order to arrive at a measure of consensus or convergence in understanding what may promote the visible unity of Christians.

Something of an analogous process is involved in inter-religious dialogue where the various religious claims of absoluteness are brought into mutual discussion. The goal, however, is not directed at unity but at understanding, corrective criticism and mutual enrichment, without diluting the respective heritages or prejudging irreducible differences. On the other hand, inter-religious dialogues do not take place in a vacuum; they are burdened by a long history of intolerance, hostility and exclusivism. In a more positive sense, they presuppose that the major religious traditions of the world have something worthwhile to contribute to the enrichment of humanity and are ways of leading people to their fulfilment — however this goal may be understood and interpreted: salvation, liberation, heaven, kingdom of God, etc. In other words the religions of the world are in some measure engaged in struggles of human fulfilment, even when these struggles are divergently expressed to the point where to outsiders they may seem merely inhuman, sub-human or super-human. In short, inter-religious encounter is an encounter between *religious* persons, each having a particular religious experience or insight into the mysteries of God or the world.

Inter-religious dialogue which takes place between religious persons does not mean, from a Christian standpoint, a surrender of our own theological conviction, nor is it an adoption of some sort of supra-sectarian viewpoint transcending all religious convictions. It does not imply either that all religions are "essentially" the same or that we must accept uncritically that everything calling itself "religion" is religious. It is in the process of dialogue that we will be able to discern the divine and the demonic in the religious commitments of people, Christians included. In a general sense, each of the major religious traditions of the world is unique, has gone through a different process of historical and cultural conditioning and has a different linguistic and fiduciary framework. What inter-religious dialogue calls for is an awareness and an openness towards the other.

Furthermore, to engage in inter-religious dialogue presupposes a clear consciousness that we live today in a religiously pluralistic world. This pluralism is not simply a sociological fact but carries with it profound theological implications as well. One significant implication of this situation is that we can no longer do Christian theology in relative isolation, or only within our own group. Christian theology has traditionally been a strictly domestic affair. And as an articulation of Christian faith and religious experience it has been based upon our attitude of religious self-sufficiency. The concerns of Christian theology have been solely dictated by its own traditions, pursued with reference to Christian canons and criteria. Christian theology seldom trespassed its own set perimeters or ventured to explore the religious convictions of others. Such tasks were left to other disciplines like the philosophy of religion or history of religions. Its primary responsibility has been to explore the fundamental Christian convictions as they evolved in the experience of the Christian community.

Our contemporary situation of religious pluralism (and the opportunity it provides for inter-religious dialogue) questions the traditional closed-shop nature of Christian theology and its attitude of a closed particularity. There is a growing recognition today that Christian theology must justify its being "Christian" by articulating a theology of religion at large and incorporating this into its traditional responsibility for its own distinctiveness. Such a theology of religion can only emerge through a process of dialogical encounters with people of other living faiths and not through an *a priori* Christian logic. The challenge before us is not one of producing a proper hypothesis which would account for the presence of religious diversity in our midst, but rather to let that diversity — with all its specific claims of religious truth and experience — question our Christian convictions and theological presuppositions. It is in this process of mutual encounter that the concerns of a Christian theology of religion become very much intertwined with the general theological task of defining Christian self-identity in the midst of others. Our own self-definition need not preclude the claims of self-identity made by other communities; in fact, a meaningful self-definition can only emerge when we see ourselves vis-à-vis others. In other words, our dialogical encounter enables us to move away from an exclusive theology of self-reference and to explore what Kenneth Cragg has called "a lively theology of cross-reference".

A dialogical theology thus implies that Christian theological reflection and articulation should be undertaken through a process of dialogue with people who hold different religious convictions. Dialogue here is not just a method of doing theology but is also a commitment to take seriously what others have to say about their beliefs and values. This commitment involves our becoming cognizant, as far as this is possible, of the religious and theological reflections of people of other faiths. In other words, a Christian theological reflection needs to take seriously the data of Christian faith but also the religious data presented by other faiths. There are indeed penetrating questions that accompany the religious data of others and demand a fresh look at our own resources.

To illustrate the point, the dialogues that have taken place between Christians and Jewish people in the post-Holocaust era have raised incisive questions which touch the heart of Christian identity. As a consequence Christian theological reflection on the Jewish people and our relations to them have become significantly different from those of our forebears; there is now a meaningful reaffirmation of certain shared spiritual values between Christians and Jews, such as a common belief in one God, our common spiritual, liturgical roots, and a shared view of history in terms of its fulfilment. Christians have now rediscovered the significance of the "Jewishness" of Jesus and this has helped them to revise stereotypical notions of Jews or Jewish groups (Pharisees) at the time of Jesus.

The kind of theological enrichment that has taken place through Christian encounter with Judaism may well also be gained through encounters with other faiths. Different religions pose different sets of questions to the content of Christian faith based upon their own religious and conceptual presuppositions. Traditionally Christianity has tended to dismiss those questions as misunderstandings or misconceptions. Today we can no longer do so. We cannot continue to pretend that the questions others pose to us hardly matter for our self-understanding. Religiously pluralistic situations implicitly and explicitly (where possible) question all claims of self-legitimation and self-sufficiency. In this process of mutual interrogation our claims for truth (and the claims of others as well) are put to the test and tempered. This enables us to sharpen our doctrinal claims, spelling them out not only in terms and categories familiar to us, but also in the language and categories intelligible to our dialogue partners. A dialogical theology therefore needs to be "multilingual" rather than "monolingual" in order to make its own claims communicable.

Inter-religious dialogue, however, is not to be understood as a form of trading our commodities, in the sense that our gospel of Christian truth credentials is somehow made negotiable under popular pressure or in pursuit of mutual relations. This could hardly be the case. No faith which enters into dialogue could take a posture of indifference to its own claims. When faiths with different claims meet and converse, their claims of finality have to be articulated anew and cannot simply be assumed. All such articulations are then tempered and chastened by the experience of dialogue. In that process not only can we make our faith and convictions communicable but even commendable to others.

In a genuine and sustained inter-religious dialogue there is every possibility that the partners will make new theological discoveries which may enhance their self-understanding and will hopefully also enable them to develop positive understanding and even appreciation of others' viewpoints. Christians would thus also be impelled to reckon with the significance of the claims that others may make for their own faith and try to find a place for those claims in Christian theological articulations without any *a priori* subordination of other faiths to the Christian self-understanding. This suggests that a dialogical theology will also need to develop certain critical principles in evaluating the claims and counter-claims made by other religions and communities and, to a certain extent, it is inevitable that these will be derived from the experience and knowledge of the Christian faith. Our own doctrinal assumptions do play a role here. Nonetheless, our critique may well turn out to be one-sided if it is based *solely* on Christian assumptions and experiences without due consideration of the historical and religious experiences of others. In short, a dialogical theology aims to enrich our self-understanding through a critical encounter without any sense of superiority or self-sufficiency.

Some implications for ecumenical theology

The preceding observations may have made it clear that a dialogical theology emerging out of Christian encounter with people of other faiths and ideologies is crucial for the formation of a Christian ecumenical theology. As indicated earlier, a truly ecumenical theology is engaged in dialogue both internally and externally — internally within the community of faith and externally with those of other faiths and no faith. These dimensions of introspection, critical analysis and open dialogue with the world would not be mutually exclusive but rather interpenetrate and shape our ecumenical self-understanding. If this assumption is correct, the adequacy of an ecumenical theology lies in its ability to relate to or address concerns of Christian faith both internally and externally. It is important, therefore, that the agenda for internal Christian discussion be not pursued without considerations of external relations. A dialogical theology arising out of Christian encounter with other faiths thus renders a service to Christian ecumenical theology by questioning its posture of self-sufficiency and closed particularity.

Secondly, it is the nature of ecumenical theology to seek new avenues of understanding. There is a genuine temptation for it to become a mere consensus theology, content to restructure the fundamentals of Christian faith in order to achieve a measure of Christian convergence. Insights derived from a dialogical theology will indeed help deepen Christian convictions. For instance, the ecumenical discussions on baptism and eucharist in recent decades would have been enriched if they had been seen in relation to, say, Hindu *samskaras*. Every internal Christian discussion, when seen against the wider background of other religious standpoints, gains new perspectives of understanding.

Thirdly, the Christian experience of dialogical encounters in different cultural and socio-political contexts raises new questions and offers new resources for ecumenical reflections. How we wrestle with those questions and how we make use of those insights and resources will determine the relevancy and adequacy of ecumenical theology. The ecumenical task is infinite; it is never finished and should never be finished.

Increasingly the task of ecumenical theology will be one of integrating and inter-relating various contextual concerns and issues of theological and practical importance in the structure of its thinking and praxis. There is every indication that in future the concerns of a dialogical theology will make a significant impact upon our collective Christian consciousness and indeed assume central importance in Christian ecumenical theology.

NOTE

[1] *Nostra Aetate*, 1965.

10. Ecumenics, Church and Society

The Tradition of Life and Work

Charles C. West

Let me set the stage with a story. Some thirty years ago when the Ecumenical Institute, Bossey, was in the excitement of its youth, I sat one day in my office with one of France's leading sociologists of the day, Prof. Henri Desroches. He had come to place our enterprise in proper perspective. "You are only one of many ecumenical movements," he pointed out. "The United Nations is one. There are cultural, religious and even technological and economic movements which in their own way are trying to bring the world together. The question you face is your place among them." He was right. Edward Schillebeeckx has put it plainly: "Considered from a sociological point, the church is only one of the social institutions of society appearing among many others and becoming by this fact an object of study for sociologists. From the sociological angle, the church presents itself in the common market of the world as a social group which works together with other groups or not at the construction of the world."[1]

Ecumenics is concerned about the world. As Christian ecumenics, it is about the world known, judged and reconciled in Christ. As such, it is missiological, dialogical, and practical. It is concerned with the way a faithful church will express the reality of Christ for the world in all of its pluralities. Teaching ecumenics, therefore, is a dialogical, sometimes a confrontational act. It involves bringing people into active encounter with one another and with the word of God as they struggle to perceive and realize the ecumenical vision.

The oikoumene

It is well known that the Greek word oikoumene means world, but in a special sense. It is the present passive participle of the verb *oikeo*, to dwell or inhabit. It refers, in contrast to the more inclusive *kosmos*, to the world of people or the inhabited world. *Kosmos* can be a metaphysical term expressing universal order or transcendent powers, demonic or divine. Oikoumene almost always refers to human dwelling, human society, and human structures as they spread over the earth.

In principle, this is a neutral concept. It was certainly so used in Matthew 24:14: "The gospel of the kingdom will be preached throughout the whole oikoumene as a testimony to all nations", and in several other passages both in the New Testament and in the Septuagint, translating the Hebrew words *tebel* or *erets*. In fact, however, the word was loaded with cultural meaning and bias. Already in the speeches of Demosthenes in fourth-century Athens, and more generally throughout the world that was Hellenized by Alexander's conquest, it signified, without surrendering its claim to universality, the world of Greek culture. "The Hellenic ideal is as such cosmopolitan, representing true humanity. Released from its local roots, it takes in the world."[2] Oikoumene slowly replaced *polis* as the focus of Greek consciousness. It was a philosophical spiritual concept of human society which reached out to pull the "barbarians" on its edges into its orbit and therefore into the meaningful world.

This was reinforced by the political development of the Roman Imperium. The two did not exactly coincide either in geography or in worldview, but they grew together slowly over the centuries into the synthesis which was given expression by Caesar Augustus, the *kurios tes oikoumenes*. In the time of Jesus the oikoumene had a political order, a cultural ethos both moral and philosophical, and a social dynamic which reached out by both force and education to bring those on its boundaries within its fold. Other peoples lived within this world, of course, with their own histories, religions and cultures. The Jews were an example. But they were included perforce in the Roman Imperium and by pervasive social pressure in a constant interaction with the Greek culture.

This oikoumene at long last fell apart as we know. Not until the twentieth century have social conditions produced anything like it again, this time without political unity and without a common culture of reference — a field of forces of which everyone is aware and which pull us, willingly or unwillingly, into dealing with each other, but whose direction and control seem beyond our powers. Nevertheless the Greco-Roman oikoumene had a profound influence on the origins of Christianity and on the mission of the church to the world ever since.

Oikoumene in Christian context

"In those days a decree went out from Caesar Augustus that all the oikoumene should be enrolled" (Luke 2:1). This is the setting for the birth of Jesus. It was the command of Caesar which brought Joseph and Mary to the place where Jewish prophecy had declared the Messiah would be born. Throughout the New Testament and the history of the early church, this political oikoumene is acknowledged as a provision of God's providence and is given at the same time a secular place in the history of salvation. The political authority of Rome is legitimated against the religious nationalism of the Jews. It is challenged to execute justice in worldly terms (John 18-19; Acts 16:19-40). The fact of the Pax Romana was understood as a providential condition for the spreading of the gospel to the ends of the earth. The church indeed in its political teachings down through the time of the Reformation assumed that political authority, however limited in practice, is in principle ecumenical, but that this ecumenicity is, at least in Western Christendom, sharply distinct from that of the church. Christians are not to worship Caesar but they are to give him his due, while expecting him to maintain justice and peace in the world.

The attitude of the New Testament towards the ecumenical culture of the time was more ambivalent. The early church lived in and expressed itself through that culture. Its freedom to do so was established by Paul's struggle against Judaizers. The New Testament could have been written in no other language than Greek, given the character of the people whose faith and story are told. Yet there was a profound truth in the complaint of the Thessalonian crowd of both Jews and Gentiles. "These men who have turned the oikoumene upside down have come here also" (Acts 17:6). The resurrection of Christ upset the balance of relations between the Jewish and the Hellenic world. The ecumenical calling of the Hebrew people, expressed so often in the psalms and in the prophets, burst free of the limits of a single nation's law. But the saving power for all peoples remains rooted in God's calling and dealing with one people whose culture was formed outside the oikoumene. Through the history of that one people fulfilled in Christ all the wisdom and all the religion of the inhabited world were called in question. "The times of ignorance God overlooked, but now he commands all men everywhere to repent because he has fixed a day on which he will judge the oikoumene in righteousness by a man whom he has appointed, and of this he has given assurance to all men by raising him from the dead" (Acts 17:30-31). The world of Hellenic culture is accepted. There is no way back into messianic nationalism. The world is at the same time judged in its ecumenical pretensions and transformed by a lord and a promise given to it from outside its own culture and religion.

To this a footnote must be added about the ends of the earth. As the church of the resurrection did not accept the limits of the Jewish law in reaching the Gentiles, so also it could not accept the limits of the Roman Imperium or the Hellenic culture in spreading the gospel. The Ethiopian eunuch (Acts 8:26ff.) is a powerful symbol. Legend has added others, bringing the apostle Thomas to India, Bartholomew and Thaddaeus to the Armenians. The vision of the Old Testament, "this is the purpose concerning the whole earth and this is the hand that is stretched out over all nations" (Isa. 14:26), is reinforced in the New. The ecumenical mission of the people of God moves beyond any conceivable limits to reach the world in all its cultures.

Thus the New Testament ecumenical vision. The conversion of the Roman Empire following Constantine introduced into it a curious ambivalence. As the Greco-Roman oikoumene was beginning to suffer invasion from outside, it was revolutionized from within by Christianity. The word ecumenical came to be applied then no longer to the work of Hellenic culture and Roman power whose limits and vulnerabilities both geographically and socially were being demonstrated every day. Nor was it extended to the barbarians of Northern Europe or the civilizations of Syria, Persia and the East. Rather it was appropriated by the church itself, or more specifically, by the church whose theology had been formed in encounter with Hellenic philosophy and whose centres of power were those of beleaguered Roman Empire. The ecumenical creeds (Apostolic, Nicean, Athanasian) and the first seven ecumenical councils expressed this ambivalence. On the one hand they defined the teaching of the church by using and transforming the categories of Greek thought. For these formulations they claimed ecumenical validity which has more or less been authoritative for the churches in Europe, their diaspora in the Americas and elsewhere, and their missions throughout the world. On the other hand, however, these creeds and councils produced a schism in the church to which the non-Chalcedonian of Egypt, Ethiopia, India and the Middle East still bear witness today. Who knows how different the history of the mission of the church to the vast oikoumene east of Jerusalem might have been had the church of the Roman Empire been less pretentious.

The ironical result of this history was a split in the Christian oikoumene itself following the seventh ecumenical council. The patriarch of Constantinople assumed the title of *ho oikoumenikos*, the ecumenical one. His successor is still known as the Ecumenical Patriarch. The pope in Rome meanwhile laid claim to the same title, and from then until the twentieth century the term ecumenical was an instrument of polemics, each side claiming ultimate validity for its interpretation of the combination of church and world. The Roman Catholic Church continued to call its councils ecumenical. The Eastern Orthodox churches had the grace not to.

The ecumenical movement

This brings us to what Archbishop William Temple has described as the great new fact of our time. Ecumenicity has become not a presumption about the church and the world but, as in the earliest centuries of the church, a movement towards the goal that Christ may take form as judge and reconciler in the whole inhabited world. It is a movement which responds to the command and promise of God which comes to us in the church. The goal may be realized provisionally at times in the church's witness or in the gift of the Spirit to an ecumenical meeting. But it is a realization known by faith, and driven by hope for what divine grace can yet achieve by human obedience and witness. Let me propose four theses concerning this history which bear upon the way ecumenics should be taught and learned today and tomorrow.

1. The modern ecumenical movement has arisen out of the command of Christ to go to the ends of the earth and make disciples of all people. When this call was taken seriously by missionaries who broke out of the confines of European-American culture, the world in all its plurality was rediscovered. In the urgency of bringing the gospel to non-Christian societies the disunity of the church in Christendom was recognized as an intolerable scandal. This recognition did not come easily or even across the world. Christians on the mission field transported the divisions and conflicts of church and society, those rooted in doctrine and those rooted in cultural bias, to the lands into which they came. These divisions took root in the new churches and had to be reconciled there. But the judgment of God on divisions and the imperative of unity in the Spirit for the sake of the church's mission itself could not be avoided. It was missionaries with this experience who organized the first modern conference called ecumenical in New York in 1900. The term was pretentious as they soon realized. It claimed ecumenicity for an evangelical fervour which was rightly suspected by other Christians for its inadequate ecclesiology. Later world conferences including those of the World Council of Churches have not assumed the title. But they have claimed something far more important, to be instruments of a movement whose aim is to seek the form of the church in its one mission to the whole world in all that world's diversity, yet calling to community in Christ. John Mackay has defined it rightly: ecumenics is "the science of the church universal conceived as a world missionary community: its nature, its functions, its relations and its strategies".[3]

2. The ecumenical movement has been characterized by a close interaction between the search for the unity of the church and the search for the form of the church which is truly missionary in every worldly situation. The faith and order movement grew out of the experience of previously suspicious churchmen at the world missionary conference in Edinburgh in 1910, an experience which one of them described as like that of a lion in a den of Daniels. It has been accompanied ever since by an awareness that the church is doubly divided: on questions of doctrine and order rooted in response to revelation, and on questions of churchmanship rooted in the language of social existence. "The Unity of the Church and the Renewal of Human Community" is the title of one of the Faith and Order movement's most recent studies. The issue is the

search for forms of worship and ministry in word, sacrament and discipline which will be faithful expressions of God's promise for all eternity. The inner ecumenics of the church and outer ecumenics of Christ's ministry to the world belong together.

3. Fundamentally the ecumenical movement has been a process of the church's rediscovery of itself and its mission on those frontiers where it has been most sharply challenged. This is the continuing excitement of the ecumenical enterprise. We can see this operating, as described above, in the Faith and Order movement. It is equally true of the other two streams which have flowed together to form the World Council of Churches.

The ecumenical experience in world mission has been one of being continually called into question by challenges to its worldly bias, and of rediscovering itself in deeper and broader terms. There were only four "younger churchmen" at Edinburgh in 1910. By the time of the Jerusalem conference in 1928, the question of Christ's relation to non-Christian religions, cultures, and secularity was the central topic of discussion with Christians native to non-Christian lands. In Tambaram in 1938 the issue was put more sharply through Hendrik Kraemer's challenging testimony to the transforming word of God in the midst of all, including Christian, religions and cultures. A revolutionary seed was planted there which bore vigorous fruit in the post-Second World War world. In the past forty years this has taken form through ecumenical challenge and dialogue, and in the shift of the base of the missionary enterprise from the traditional Christian lands to the churches in all parts of the world. It has led to profound struggles which are still going on to discern the judgment and grace of God in the midst of revolutions, struggles for liberation and efforts by nations to find their social identity amid the changing powers of an interdependent world. The question: Who are the people of God for a world in this ferment?, is the critical, missiological and ecumenical question today. What repentance, what renewal, what form of the gospel, special to each place yet faithful to the church ecumenical, is called for?

The Life and Work movement has a similar history. Already from Stockholm 1925 to Oxford 1937 a shift took place from the articulation of Christian ideals to be realized everywhere to a searching analysis of the conflicts and powers of a world poised on the brink of war, the involvement of churches with those powers, and the judging and redeeming word of God to both church and world. The slogan of Oxford, "Let the church be the church", was a call to the churches away from false entanglements to a true ecumenicity. With this the ground was laid for the social witness of the World Council of Churches in the post-war years that followed. It was a dialogical witness at every stage, first under the heading of "responsible society" then, with the addition of concern for non-human creation, "just, participatory and sustainable society", and most recently "justice, peace and the integrity of creation". A solid base of ecumenical teaching on social questions has emerged from this problem, but it has continually been called in question and reformulated by the challenge of the new participants in the dialogue and new urgencies in social action. The dialogue still continues, often between Christians on opposite sides of intense, sometimes even violent, social conflict, who wrestle with each other's souls for the true form of the social witness of the church.

4. The ecumenical movement has always involved a struggle for the discernment of faith in a world of ideological conflict. This was already involved in Karl Barth's

massive challenge to the culture Christianity of his time. It was central to Kraemer's work as well, and to the struggles of the Confessing Church in Nazi Germany. After the Second World War, it emerged in a continuing Christian encounter with the challenge of Marxism and with the temptations of a prosperous capitalism in the West. More recently it has been expressed in the search for forms of Christian self-understanding in emerging nations becoming more conscious of their identities in renascent non-Christian ideological terms. Ideologies are coherent structures of ideas used to understand the forces at work in a society in terms which lead to definite strategies of social action aiming at defined goals of human fulfilment. The demand for total commitment is implicit in them. Yet some ideological substance is present in all engaged human thought, including that of Christians. How does the gospel use, judge and transform ideology in seeking the form of its ecumenical witness and action? This too is continuing agenda of the ecumenical movement.

Ecumenics as a dialogical discipline

What then does all this imply for the way in which we teach ecumenics and involve our students in it? Fundamentally it means that ecumenics cannot be taught descriptively as a subject matter to be grasped and stored in the mind. It begins when the believer finds him- or herself engaged in an ecumenical context, with the challenge to life and faith which this involves. Our first teaching act must be, therefore, to place our students in such a context or to make them aware of the way in which they are already ecumenically challenged. For example,

1. This involves awareness of oneself and one's location in church and in world. It means that what one has taken for granted there must be brought to consciousness and examined. Many have had such experiences when their assumptions about society or about mission were called into question by fellow Christians with deeper experiences and better formulated ideas. It has been said that an ecumenical experience of this kind can reinforce the theological or social divisions by refining them in the encounter, and indeed this can sometimes happen. But usually this occurs when the context is missing of a mutual commitment to one another as Christians, based on an awareness, spoken or unspoken, that God is judge and redeemer of us all. When this context is present, it can not only deepen our understanding in unity, but also extend to non-believers who challenge us better to understand ourselves in faith.

2. The second step in ecumenical study is the struggle of Christians with each other for the form of true faith and witness. It is an axiom of the ecumenical movement that no participant is asked to surrender or prescind from basic convictions about faith or life. Every ecumenical meeting is therefore an encounter, the results of which cannot be foreseen and whose success cannot be guaranteed. Every ecumenical consensus is the work of the Holy Spirit changing human perspectives as they argue with one another in the presence of God. In extreme cases in the history of the church, most recently the so-called German Christians with their pro-Nazi distortion of the gospel, and the white Dutch Reformed Churches of South Africa in their acceptance of apartheid, this struggle has come to an ecumenical decision to condemn the doctrine and suspend contacts. But even this action is a form of ecumenical relations. It involves a call for repentance and a commending of the action of the church to the merciful judgment of God. Christians in ecumenical encounter do not compromise with conscience or with faithful witness, but neither do they absolutize the oikoumene.

3. Ecumenics involves continuing penultimate action by Christians in the world's struggles for justice and peace even when these actions may cause division in the churches. It involves at the same time openness to God's judgment and correction through the ecumenical encounter. The critical question for prayer and study, therefore, is: How are we being transformed in our encounter with the world as we prepare the way for the coming of Christ?[4] What is the role of other Christians of different ideologies and different action commitments in this transformation? We are actors on the ecumenical stage. There is no way we can escape responsibility for our acts. There is no retreat into another world. Precisely in the church we are also worldly. This the ecumenical movement brings home in full force. How then can we bear witness to the judgment and forgiveness of God on even the rightness of our actions and thus be trustworthy brothers and sisters in Christ to those who are injured by what we responsibly do, or who believe we are wrong in doing it? How can our penultimate responsible actions bear witness to the ultimate reconciling work of Christ? This question is the open-ended stimulus and promise of ecumenical encounter.

Teaching method in ecumenics

Let me close with a few more practical suggestions. They presuppose a classroom with theological students, which is my own experience. The overarching question at the top of every syllabus is the simple one: What is our mission as Christians in the world? How do we discern the encounter of God with the church and the world where we exercise our responsibility? Then follow at least four steps.

1. Presentation of the ideological challenge of the world to Christian faith and understanding. This may, in different courses, be Marxism, free enterprise ideology, or various forms of scientific or technological worldviews. The challenge of renascent religious ideologies in Islam, Hinduism, Buddhism, Shinto and the like, I must leave to my colleague in the history of religions who has specialized in these fields. In many cases I try to bring these worldly structures of thought and action into dialogue with Christian theologians or philosophers who have taken them seriously or who have made their own syntheses of theology and philosophy. Most of these in recent generations have been participants in the ecumenical dialogue and have contributed substantially to it.

2. I try as far as possible to bring the contrast and conflict among Christians into the classroom itself. This can often be done by calling on students from overseas, for Princeton Seminary is rich in ecumenical fellowship on campus itself. As supplement or substitute, however, there are books that present the challenges with which we should be wrestling. It is an exceptional course in theology or ethics at Princeton in the past few years which does not include some reading in black theology, in liberation theology, and in feminist perspectives. Out of personal experience and interest I try to add Asian perspectives which fit none of these categories. The reaction of students is different to various of these stimuli. Sometimes the instructor must act as the protagonist for an uncomfortable or unfamiliar point of view.

3. I try to encourage students to rethink their own traditions and their own convictions, theological and social, in the light of the encounter in the class. Sometimes this involves he or she digging more deeply into a position espoused but not adequately understood. At other times it means exploring a new enthusiasm critically. I expect every paper to be a critical dialogue.

4. Finally I ask students to project ecumenical policy and action for the church. I ask them to test this policy in the light of its critics and possible alternatives. In the ideal case a student may him- or herself have been involved in action on some frontier or can become involved as part of the course itself. Even if this is not the case, there is enough in every student's experience and imagination to make such a projection possible.

A final word. Ecumenics is an ongoing event. The fruits which it produces — reports of conferences, examples of faithful witness by churches or persons whether with or against the consensus of fellow believers, and new creeds and practices within the church — are all interesting and important, but they are not in themselves the object of study. Rather the process itself is the real subject matter: the encounter between living traditions and involved Christians struggling and working with one another. It is important for students to study the history of this process in order that they themselves may become a part of it. But the object of teaching ecumenics is to involve them as participants.

NOTES

[1] *Oecumenica: an Annual Symposium of Ecumenical Research*, 1969, Kantzenbach and Vajta eds, p.180.
[2] *Theologisches Wörterbuch des Neuen Testaments*, Fünfter Band, p.159.
[3] *Ecumenics: the Science of the Church Universal*, 1964, p.27.
[4] As many will recognize, I am using here the terms of Dietrich Bonhoeffer, *Ethics*, chapters IV and V.

PART II

Reports of
Working Groups

11. The Teaching of Ecumenics

Introduction

The reflections of this group on the teaching of ecumenics identify as the aims of this enterprise:
1) to construct a biblical and theological foundation for the ecumenical vision itself;
2) to keep vital and alive the ecumenical memory which has directed and shaped the movement from its inception;
3) to encourage and foster a new generation of ecumenical thinkers and workers for the churches.

Methodological considerations

I. Some issues

In order to succeed in the teaching of ecumenics, it is helpful to encourage the student to make some personal reflection on his or her own ecumenical journey, prior to the commencement of study, and perhaps be prepared to share these reflections with the other students. The following issues might be expected to inform this early discussion:
1) biblical interpretation and vision
2) theological and institutional context
3) personal commitment to the ecumenical task
4) personal historical perspective and involvements

II. Learning/teaching suggestions

Once the students have had a chance to reflect on their own experiences in ecumenism, it is helpful to encourage reading and reflection on some basic introductory works (see bibliography), and to invite students to relate such reading to developments in their own regions and contexts. The following questions might prove helpful for discussion:
1. How are contextual issues of tension, conflict, brokenness reflected in local ecumenical and interchurch expressions of hymnody, church life, biblical studies and educational programmes?
2. What do we mean/understand by the use of the term "oikoumene"? By phrases such as "the responsible society", "all in each place", "unity of humankind", "justice, peace and the integrity of creation", and other ecumenical catch-words?

3. What does our own experience and contextual understanding lead us to identify as the classical or universal "marks" or signs of the institutional church? Of the ecumenical church?

Tentative outline of course

After a preliminary engagement of one another around some general themes of the ecumenical movement, the following outline of a course on ecumenical thought and practice may be implemented:

I. Introduction
1) Sharing of ecumenical journeys
2) Discussion on areas of agreement/disagreement, and sharing of reflection on the contextual nature of experience in the ecumenical movement

II. Differing ecclesial visions
1. Describing different approaches to the meaning of church
    a) church as holy and apostolic
    b) church as confessing and ethically engaged
    c) case studies:
        — interchurch dialogue in Asia
        — twentieth-century liturgical renewal movements
        — the Barmen Declaration of 1934 and the German "Confessing Church"
        — Latin American base communities and the movement for liberation
        — the Second Vatican Council as a new ecclesiological vision for the Roman Catholic Church

2. Theological visions informing ecumenism
    a) Biblical themes
        — God the Creator
        — covenant theology
        — the nature of the Trinity
        — the centrality of Jesus in the life of the church — kenotic Christianity
    b) Convergence thinking on doctrinal matters
        — BEM
        — the community of women and men in the church
        — convergence on mission and evangelism
    c) New visions since Vancouver

III. Non-theological factors in church unity and division
1) Human brokenness and the divisions of the church
2) Political ideologies and church division
3) Non-theological impulses which assist the ecumenical movement
4) Economic issues (international debt, multinational corporations, etc.)

IV. Missionary perspectives on ecumenism
1. Historical overview
    a) the international missionary conferences

b) modern mission convergence (1982)
c) joint-venture ecumenism and sharing of resources
d) third-world missionary enterprises
2. Ecumenism and dialogue with other living faiths

V. Ecumenical spirituality and praying for unity

VI. Case studies in ecumenism

1. NATIONAL AND REGIONAL EXPERIENCES

a) India

Emphases in this regional study might include: material on the Church of South India and the Church of North India, the movements of Indian Christians in the nineteenth and twentieth centuries to seek church unity, the contemporary discussions in India involving Lutherans and the Mar Thoma Church, questions of church and society, and interfaith dialogue.

The process of examining church union schemes should highlight the theological perspectives as well as the so-called non-theological factors which help or hinder such movements towards union.

b) Korea

This case study concentrates on the coming together of Christians and Buddhists, and Christians among themselves, in the attempt to work together for liberation. Key dates in this story are 1895, 1919, 1960 and 1970. Included in the study is information on the contribution of missionaries in the movement towards unity and the situation of division among Christians. Political, social, economic and theological factors in the movement towards unity and the state of division are also examined. Resource materials might include: Kim Yong Bock, *Minjung Theology*, New York, Orbis Press; Cyris H.S. Moon, *A Korean Minjung Theology: an Old Testament Perspective*, New York, Orbis Press, 1985; *International Review of Mission*, spring 1985.

c) Nigeria

This case study would examine the attempts to manifest Christian unity in Nigeria. Resources might include: Ogbu U. Kalu, *Divided People of God: Church Union Movement in Nigeria, 1875-1966*, New York, NOK Publishing Ltd, 1978.

d) Madagascar

This study would endeavour to interpret some of the basic characteristics of a successful ecumenical effort in a non-Western setting in which at least three factors have played a decisive role. The first factor is the emancipation movement of local churches in relationship to their parent missionary bodies; the second, the process of nation-building and the role of Christianity in it; finally, better stewardship of existing resources used in performing missionary tasks. The Church of Jesus Christ in Madagascar was established in 1968 in a merger of Congregationalist, Reformed and Quaker church bodies. Resource material might include the newsletter of the Church since 1969/1970, *Vaovao* FJKM (international edition in French and English); Victor Rakotoarimanana, "Le problème des négociations d'union en Afrique", *Foi et vie*, 64,

1965, pp.58-75; "Confession of Faith in the Church of Jesus Christ in Madagascar", in *Reformed Witness Today*, L. Vischer, ed., Bern, 1982.

e) The United Kingdom

This case study would be an example of a North Atlantic attempt to overcome the divisions later exported to other continents. It would explore the various efforts to achieve Christian unity in the United Kingdom in light of the Nottingham Faith and Order conference of 1964; the multilateral conversations in Scotland; the Covenanting Agreement in Wales; the Anglican-Methodist conversations; the formation of the United Reformed Churches; the Ten Propositions and responses to them; the churches covenanting for unity. To be noted in this study are the non-doctrinal factors, especially the tension between the episcopal and other ecclesiastical polities. Material might include: John Huxtable, *New Hope for Christian Unity*, Glasgow, Fount, 1977; Martin Conway, *Unity — Why not Yet?*, London, BCC, 1980.

The above examples are simply intended to illustrate the kind of approaches that can be taken in the development of studies in particular regions. Other examples would include: Australia, Central Africa (especially Uganda), the Caribbean, Latin America, the United States (especially the Consultation on Church Union), and Eastern Europe.

2. CASE STUDY: THE ORTHODOX

Dealing with the role of the Orthodox churches in the ecumenical movement requires a basic knowledge of these churches and their place in the Greek and Roman oikoumene. The early Christian councils would have to be explored and the schisms identified including Chalcedon in 451 and the later division between Rome and Byzantium in 1054. The attempts to restore unity would be examined through the use of resources such as the *Henotikon* of Zeno of 482 (text in Bettenson, *Documents of the Christian Church*, pp.123-126), the "Three Chapters" of 553 (text *ibid.*, pp.126-128), monothelitism (cf. *ibid.*, p.128), and other attempts by both Rome and Byzantium during the Middle Ages.

Basic Orthodox theology and tradition would be studied with an accent on spirituality and liturgical life. If ecumenics in the Middle East were taken as an example, special attention would have to be given to the role of the regional councils or conferences: Conference of the Heads of Oriental Orthodox Churches (Addis Ababa, 1965); the Middle East Council of Churches which was established in 1974; the All Africa Conference of Churches established in 1963.

The bilateral dialogues are of cardinal importance for the Orthodox. In addition to the dialogues with the Anglican communion, the Lutheran communion and other Protestant churches, careful attention should be given to the Roman Catholic and the Uniate churches, the dialogue between the Roman Catholic and individual Orthodox churches such as the Syrian, Coptic and the Ecumenical Patriarchate, and of course the dialogue between the Chalcedonian (Byzantine) and the Non-Chalcedonian (Oriental) Orthodox churches. Suggested resource material is included in the bibliography.

VII. Field work

It is strongly recommended that all students enter into the life of a religious or Christian tradition other than their own for the purpose of examining the tensions in society and among themselves as they commit themselves to the ecumenical cause. Attention should be paid to the signs of conversion, renewal and hope in the midst of these conflicts. Problems relating to mixed marriages, differing interpretations of domestic and international affairs as well as questions of racism and sexism should be examined in light of their impact upon the churches. It is important that regular occasions for rep that regular occasions for reflecting upon these experiences are provided.

Selected basic reading

"Baptism, Eucharist and Ministry", *Faith and Order Paper No. 111*, Geneva, WCC, 1982.

Bent, Ans van der, *A Guide to Essential Ecumenical Reading*, Geneva, WCC, 1984.

Bent, Ans van der, *What in the World is the World Council of Churches?*, Geneva, WCC, 1978.

Birmele, André, ed., *Local Ecumenism*, Geneva, WCC, 1984, and *In Each Place*, Geneva, WCC, 1977.

Boff, Leonardo, *Ecclesiogenesis*, New York, Orbis Press, 1985.

Bria, Ion, *Go Forth In Peace: Orthodox Perspectives on Mission*, Geneva, WCC, 1986.

Crow, Paul, *Christian Unity: Matrix for Mission*, New York, Friendship Press, 1982.

Mission and Evangelism: an Ecumenical Affirmation, 1982, Geneva, WCC, 1982.

Vischer, Lukas and Meyer Harding, eds, *Growth in Agreement*, New York, Paulist Press, 1984.

Selected bibliography

"Baptism, Eucharist and Ministry" *Faith and Order Paper No. 111*, Geneva, WCC, 1982.

Bent, Ans van der, *A Guide to Essential Ecumenical Reading*, Geneva, WCC, 1984.

Bent, Ans van der, *What in the World is the World Council of Churches?*, Geneva, WCC, 1978.

Boff, Leonardo, *Ecclesiogenesis*, New York, Orbis Press, 1985.

Bria, Ion, *Go Forth in Peace: Orthodox Perspectives on Mission*, Geneva, WCC, 1986.

Degrijae, O., *La tierce Eglise missionnaire*.

Dulles, Avery, *Models of the Church*, Dublin, Gill & MacMillan, 1974.

Dulles, Avery, *The Catholicity of the Church*, Oxford, Oxford Press, 1986.

Evdokimov, Paul, *L'orthodoxie*, Neuchâtel/Paris, Delachaux et Niestlé, 1959.

For All God's People, Geneva, WCC, 1982.

Fouilloux, E., *Les catholiques et l'unité chrétienne du XIXe au XXe siècle*, Paris, Centurion, 1982.

Gill, David, ed. *Gathered for Life*, Geneva, WCC, 1983.

Gregorios, Paulos, Lazareth, William and Nissiotis, Nikos, eds, *Does Chalcedon Divide or Unite?*, Geneva, WCC, 1981.

Inter-Orthodox Symposium on Baptism, Eucharist and Ministry, Geneva, WCC, 1986.

Keyes, Lawrence E., *The Last Age of Missions*, Pasadena, Williams Carey Library, 1983.

Les Editions du Centre orthodoxe, Chambésy, *Etudes théologiques*:

1. *Eglise locale et Eglise universelle*, 1981.
2. *Le IIe Concile oecuménique: signification et actualité pour le monde chrétien d'aujourd'hui*, 1982.
3. *Luther et la réforme allemande dans une perspective oecuménique*, 1983.
4. *La théologie dans l'Eglise et dans le monde*, 1984.
5. *Les dialogues oecuméniques hier et aujourd'hui*, 1986.

Lossky, Vladimir, *The Mystical Theology of the Eastern Church*, London, J. Clarke, 1957.

Lossky, Vladimir, *Orthodox Theology, an Introduction*, Crestwood, NY, St Vladimir's Press, 1978.

Lossky, Vladimir, *The Vision of God*, New York, St Vladimir's Seminary Press, 1983.

Martensen, Daniel F., ed., "Quest for Consensus", *Journal of Ecumenical Studies*, Philadelphia, Temple University, summer 1986.

Matthews, John, *The Unity Scene*, London, BCC, 1986.

Meyendorff, John, *Byzantine Theology*, New York, St Vladimir's Seminary Press, 1975.

Meyendorff, John, *St Gregory Palamas and Orthodox Spirituality*, New York, St Vladimir's Seminary Press, 1974.

Moltmann, Jürgen, *The Trinity and the Kingdom of God*, London, SCM, 1981.

Rouse, R. and Neill, S. *The History of the Ecumenical Movement,* Vol. I, London, SPCK, 1954.

Schmemann, Alexander, *For the Life of the World*, New York, National Student Christian Federation, 1963.

Staniloae, Dimitru, *Theology and the Church*, New York, St Vladimir's Seminary Press, 1980.

Vischer, Lukas, *Intercession*, Geneva, WCC, 1980.

Vischer, Lukas, and Meyer, Harding, eds, *Growth in Agreement*, New York, Paulist Press, 1984.

Visser 't Hooft, W.A., *The Meaning of Ecumenical*, Geneva, WCC, 1954.

Ware, Timothy, *The Orthodox Church*, Harmondsworth, Penguin Books, 1967.

Weber, Hans-Ruedi, *Asia and the Ecumenical Movement*, London, SCM, 1966.

12. Models of Christian Unity

Introduction

This paper concerns itself with several models of Christian unity as a point of departure in teaching about ecumenics, as a way of engaging learners in the central task of Christian unity, and as a means of bringing students to the forefront of the ecumenical enterprise.

I. Aims

The aims of utilizing models of Christian unity in teaching ecumenics are:
1) to assist in diagnosing the divisions and brokenness of human community
2) to conceptualize the issues and arrangements by which unity may be achieved in ecclesial terms
3) to provide a way of visualizing the ecumenical endeavour as a whole
4) as a convenient "window on the church" providing a focus for theological scrutiny and biblical justification, as well as reflection on such current issues as ecclesial integrity, authority, power, structure, etc.

II. Uses

To pursue ecumenics via models requires that teachers (and students) recognize the premises and aims of the schema of models utilized and clarify their own purposes in investigating them.

First, delineation of models might be undertaken for normative or theological reasons. Biblical or exegetical theology might examine the whole issue of unity and diversity and elaborate Old or New Testament types of the church. A different set of normative models could be generated by systematic inquiry into the visions of and hopes for unity nurtured by the several confessional families. Second, historical research would require models appropriate to the period and area under investigation. Quite an elaborate scheme — perhaps more of a catalogue — might be needed to embrace the range of twentieth-century experiments in Christian unity and of efforts at unity through the whole history of the church. Such an approach would, in all probability, be unconcerned about the current viability or theological integrity of the models discerned. The same could be said of a third use, for the social sciences. Sociology might well conceptualize Christian unity in a fashion comparable to its handling of religious movements (church, denomination, sect, etc.), that is, analytically and abstractly, ordering various relationships, factors, patterns into ideal types. In current ecumenical dialogues, models serve a fourth purpose, one that might be termed constructive or programmatic. Paul Crow's criteria for identifying and including models illustrate this use. He sought models that were current, that were perceived by representatives of the churches to be viable and that deliberately witnessed to the unity of the church.

Methodological considerations

I. Some issues

In principle, a course on models of Christian unity could explore the entire ecumenical terrain. Certain issues, however, are sharpened viewed in relation to models:

1) unity and mission
2) how unity expresses itself in structure and order
3) the relation of diversity (theological, ecclesiastical, cultural) to unity
4) solidarity, catholicity, conciliarity
5) implications of models of unity for the church, local, regional, universal
6) marks of the church in relation to unity
7) unity of the church and the unity of humankind
8) ministry for unity and Petrine ministry
9) unity and divergent linguistic and value systems, understandings and world-views
10) models of unity offered from the Orthodox perspective

II. Learning/teaching suggestions

Models of unity will focus on ecclesiological and ethical issues if they become living options. To that end, the learning context should be so constructed that models become more than sophisticated academic concepts to be played against each other in an intellectual and abstract thought game. Students should:

1) experience the disunity of the church and brokenness of the world, confronting the problems before attempting solutions for them
2) encounter human diversity — different peoples, languages, ecclesial traditions, perspectives (male, female; rich, poor; lay, clergy; third-world, first-world) preferably within the course itself
3) attempt to assume a cultural, social and ecclesial stance radically different from their own and to reflect on at least one model from that stance
4) take critical account of the cultural and confessional context of each model and the historical circumstances that motivate its sense of the scandal of division
5) participate, actually or vicariously, in some experiment in church unity, perhaps some pioneering venture not fully embraced by the current models
6) come to a decision, even if tentative, on a preferred model of Christian unity
7) advocate that model in a context for which the student has some responsibility (perhaps by drafting a policy statement which calls upon a local church or regional church body to take steps towards visible unity)
8) explain the decision and action to students who have taken different positions and who represent different cultural and ecclesial traditions (typically, to other members of the course)

III. Critical questions

To assist teachers or students to use this paper or others identified in the bibliography below, a few critical questions should be raised. Some apply with greatest force to the scheme of models as a whole, others might be pursued with each model.

1) How credibly do the schema and individual models disclose the radical divisions and brokenness of human community? Do these attempts at a Christian answer address the questions posed by the human condition?

2) In what sense are the models or the schema a reflection of the diversity of cultures, races, traditions? How natural, value-free and universal are they? Will the schema, for instance, work readily in the various Christian cultures, or does it have a North Atlantic bias?

3) In what sense would women recognize these analyses as aptly diagnosing Christian divisions and Christian unity (the poor)?

4) Does the schema seem to be patterned on a particular tradition, to represent a specific theological way of viewing reality? Would the Orthodox, for instance, concede its accuracy?

5) Is it constructed in such a way as to favour one model over others?

6) How is the schema (or the models individually) oriented towards change? Is it, for instance, specific to the twentieth-century (or to other particular centuries)? Is it, in principle, static or open? Can the schema or the individual models be adjusted as context and circumstances alter? Or, to put the matter in a more normative fashion, are the models individually and collectively understood as provisional?

7) How inclusive is it? Have the criteria for or marks of a model been delineated in such a way as to exclude what could be regarded as important directions towards Christian unity?

8) How is the schema oriented towards issues of mission? Are the models understood as ends or means? Is unity conceived in the schema as a whole or in particular models as ends to be pursued in their own right, or as instrumental towards some other end?

9) What particular experiences of disunity or disorder — what sense of scandal — inform the models?

10) What are the ecclesial presuppositions of various models or of the schema as a whole? What are deemed the essential characteristics or elements for a model of Christian unity? What should be the test of its adequacy?

11) How does the schema treat contextual matters?

12) Does it pertain to the relationship of Christianity to other religions?

13) How are the models understood in relation to one another? As alternatives? As intermediate stages? As mutually reinforcing, compatible?

Tentative outline of course

INTRODUCTION

A course on models of Christian unity might well be structured according to one of the following approaches or embrace several:

1) Chronological, following the development of models of unity in the Faith and Order papers or through a deeper enquiry into the Christian past

2) Bilateral and multilateral, using particular dialogues as a means of access to wider ecumenical conversations
3) Issue-oriented (see above)
4) Case-study, perhaps involving a contrast of a CEB (Base Christian Community) with an experiment in unity from another context
5) Exegetical/biblical, exploring the models on that basis
6) Regional, perhaps focusing on a united and uniting church from some other continent (e.g. South India if the class is European)
7) Systematic, ecclesiological, perhaps discerning in selected ecclesiologies the essential elements for unity as a first step towards a theological assessment of existing models of unity

A COURSE ON MODELS FOR CHRISTIAN UNITY

I. Participatory phase
1) Sending of students to observe churches other than their own (including Orthodox, Roman Catholic and Protestant churches) in order to experience their worship, witness and work and to interview ministers and laity from those churches
2) Sending of students to situations where the political, social and economic divisions of human community are clearly manifested and intensively experienced
3) Reflecting together on the experiences of human division and confessional difference
4) Drawing conclusions from these experiences concerning the nature and cause of disunity as well as the churches' emerging unity
(Teachers may wish to structure the participatory phase as ongoing and continuous with the latter two phases.)

II. Academic phase
1) Defining the ecumenical problems, unity, diversity, division, ecumenism
2) Exploring the history of the church with concentration on models of unity and attempts towards unity
  unity and disunity
    in the New Testament/Old Testament
    early church (first through fifth centuries)
    medieval period
    Reformation through eighteenth century
    nineteenth century
    twentieth century
3) Examining the contemporary context — the churches' unity in relation to the unity of humankind
4) Reviewing and evaluating current models of unity (e.g. organic unity, conciliar fellowship, reconciled diversity, communion of communions, unity as solidarity)
5) Delineating ecclesiological criteria for models of the church, for instance:
  — criteria for being true to the gospel
  — those dimensions which allow the church to be a sign of the renewal of human community
  — preference for a model of unity for the whole church

— the degree to which models give expression to those significant and determinative features of the several types of churches

III. Practical phase

Giving students the opportunity to take part in a concrete project in their own situations (as outlined methodology above) or beyond their situation in some significant ecumenical venture.

Suggested basic reading

C.C.C., *The Failure of the English Covenant*, London, BCC/CCC, 1982.
C.C.C., *Towards Visible Unity: Proposals for a Covenant*, London, CCC, 1980.
Conway, Martin ed., *Unity — Why Not Yet?*, London, BCC, 1980.
Haggart, Alastair (foreword), *Essays on the Covenant*, London, BCC, 1982.
Huxtable, John, *New Hope for Christian Unity*, Glasgow, Fount, 1977.
Huxtable, John and P.C. Rodger, *Visible Unity: Ten Propositions*, London, Churches' Unity Commission, 1976.
> Responses to the Propositions from Catholic Bishops' Conference of England and Wales (1977), from United Reformed Church (1978), from Church of England General Synod — G.S. 300, 300A, 300B, 373, 473, G.S. Misc. 76.
Leonard, G. et al, *The Covenant: a Re-assessment*, London, CLS, 1981.
Montefiori, H. and L. Newbigin, *Can We Covenant?*, Leeds, John Paul Press, 1981.
Song, C.S. *Growing Together into Unity*, Geneva, WCC, 1978.
Zizioulas, John "The Ecclesiology of the Orthodox Tradition", *Search*, 7, 2, 1984, pp.42-52.

Selected bibliography

Archbishops' Commission on Doctrine, *Christian Believing*, London, SPCK, 1976.
Barrett, C.K. *The First Epistle to the Corinthians*, London, A. & C. Black, 196?
Beardslea, John W. (III), *Reformed Dogmatics*, New York, OUP, 1965 (Johannes Wollebius p.29).
Best, Ernest, *Commentary on I and II Thessalonians*, London, A. & C. Black, 196?.
Bonhoeffer, Dietrich, *Ethics*, London, SCM, 1955.
Buchsel, Friedrich, "Tradition", in Theologisches Wörterbuch zum Neuen Testament, LL, pp.171ff. *op. cit.*
CEC, "Churches in Conciliar Fellowship", *Occasional Paper No. 10*, Geneva, Conference of European Churches, 1978.
Church of Scotland, *What Keeps Churches Apart?*, Edinburgh, St Andrew Press, 1956.
Cochrane, Arthur, *Reformed Confessions of the Sixteenth Century*, London, SCM, 1966.
"Confessing Our Faith Around the World", Geneva, WCC, *Faith and Order Papers* 104, 120, 123.
Congar, Yves, *Diversity and Communion*, London, SCM, 1984.
Congar, Yves, *Tradition and Traditions*, London, Burns & Oates, 1966.
Conzelmann, Hans, *1 Corinthians*, Philadelphia, Fortress, 1979.
Derr, T.S., *Barriers to Ecumenism*, New York, Orbis, 1983.
Duchrow, Ulrich, *Conflict over the Ecumenical Movement*, Geneva, WCC, 1981.
Falconer, Alan, ed., *Understanding Human Rights*, Dublin, Irish School of Ecumenics, 1980.
Flannery, A., *op. cit.*, *Divine Revelation, Decree on Ecumenism*.
Forell, G. & J. McCue, eds, *Confessing One Faith* (pp.39-62, article by W. Kasper), Minneapolis, Augsburg, 1982.
Gassmann, G. and N. Ehrenstrom, *Confessions in Dialogue*, Geneva, WCC, 1975.

Gassmann, Gunther and Harding Meyer, *The Unity of the Church*, Geneva, LWF, 1983, LWF Report No. 15.

Gremillion, Joseph, *The Gospel of Peace and Justice*, New York, Orbis, 1976.

Grenholm, Carl-Henry, *Christian Social Ethics in a Revolutionary Age*, Uppsala, Verbum, 1973.

Haverwas, Stanley, *A Community of Character: Toward a Constructive Social Ethic*, London, University of Notre Dame, 1981.

Højen, P. *Ecumenical Methodology*, Geneva, LWF, 1978.

Hudson, Darril, *The WCC in International Affairs*, Leighton Buzzard, Faith Press, 1977.

Kane, Margaret, *Gospel in Industrial Society*, London, SCM, 1980.

Koinonia of the Paradosis — the Church as the Confessing Community.

Koinonia of the Paradosis — the Church as the Loving Community

Kung, H. & J. Moltmann eds, *An Ecumenical Confession of Faith?*, New York, Seabury, Edinburgh, T. & T. Clark, 1979 & *Concilium* 18.

Lehmann, Paul, *Ethics in a Christian Context*, New York, Harper, 1963.

Link, Hans-Georg, "Apostolic Faith Today", *Faith and Order Paper No. 124*, Geneva, WCC, 1985.

Littell & Locke eds, *The German Church Struggle and the Holocaust*, Detroit, Wayne State University Press, 1974, especially article by A.C. Cochrane.

LWF, *The Identity of the Church*, 2 vols. Geneva, LWF, 197?.

McDonagh, Enda, *Invitation and Response*, Dublin, Gill & Macmillan, 1972.

McNeill, J. and J. Nichols, *Ecumenical Testimony*, Philadelphia, Westminster, 1974.

Moltmann, Jurgen, *The Church in the Power of the Spirit*, London, SCM, 1975.

Moltmann, Jurgen, *The Open Church*, London, SCM, 1978.

Niebuhr, Richard, *Social Sources of Denominationalism*, New York, Meridian, 1957.

Nissiotis, Nikos, "The Unity of Scripture and Tradition", *Greek Orthodox Theological Review*, 11, 2, 65/66, pp.187ff.

Paton, David, *Breaking Barriers*, Nairobi Assembly report, London, SPCK, 1976.

Pradervand, M., *A Century of Service*, Edinburgh, St Andrew Press, 1977.

Puglisi, J. and S.J. Voico, *A Bibliography of Interchurch and Interconfessional Theological Dialogues*, Rome, Centro pro Unione, 1984.

Richey, Russell, *Denominationalism*, Nashville, Abingdon, 1977.

Richey, Russell, *Journal of Ecumenical Studies*, 16, 2, 1979.

Shinn, Roger, ed., *Church and Society: Ecumenical Perspectives*, Geneva, WCC, 1985.

Tillard, Jean, "What is the Church of God?", *One in Christ*, 20, 3, 1984, pp.226-242.

Vanier, Jean, *Community and Growth*, London, DLT, 1979.

Vatican Secretariat for Promoting Christian Unity, *Ecumenical Collaboration, at the National, Regional and Local Level*, London, CTS, 1975.

Vischer, Lukas, *The Confession of a Common Faith*, Geneva, WCC, 1980.

Vischer, Lukas, *Documentary History*, *op. cit.*, Lund.

Vischer, Lukas, *A Documentary History of the Faith and Order Movement 1927-1963*. St Louis, Missouri, Bethany Press, 1963.

Vischer, Lukas, *Documentary History*, Toronto Statement.

Vischer, Lukas, Louvain, Accra and Bangalore, *ops cit*.

Vischer, Lukas, ed., "What Kind of Unity?" *Faith and Order Paper No. 69*, Salamanca Report, Geneva, WCC, 1974.

Vorgrimler, H. ed, *Commentary on the Documents of Vatican II*, Fribourg, Herder, 1968, Vol. 11.

Ware, Kallistos, "What is a Martyr?", *Sobornost*, 7, 1, 1983, pp.7-18.

WCC, *All in Each Place*, Geneva, WCC, 1977.

WCC, papers on "Non Theological Factors", *Faith and Order Paper No. 2*, Geneva, WCC, 1952.

Winter, Michael, *Mission or Maintenance?*, London, DLT, 1973.

13. Teaching the Bible in Ecumenical Perspective

Introduction

This group gave careful consideration to several issues of concern to those who would seek to incorporate ecumenical perspectives into the teaching of the Old and New Testaments. It developed some general guidelines to inform all teaching of the Bible, and identified some special issues of contemporary concern for this theme. In principle the course outline which follows the first two sections of the report would provide a skeletal outline for an introductory course of biblical study in ecumenical perspective, but it should also be possible to incorporate the ecumenical perspectives contained in this report into any existing course of study.

Guidelines

1. The Bible is a living and liberating book. It should be taught and studied as such. Examples of the vital and liberating use of scripture can be seen in the Minjung theology in Korea, in certain aspects of the struggle for liberation in South Africa, in the survival of the church in China since 1949. In Western societies the task of teaching the Bible doubtless requires a reassessment of these living and liberating elements, particularly in the light of the flagrant misuse of scripture in support of expanding militarism or wasteful and thoughtless consumption of the world's resources. An ecumenical framework of teaching provides a basis upon which to distinguish between good and bad uses of the Bible. Indeed, we may be able to use the Bible itself to enhance the ecumenical dialogue, by studying its internal conflicts and confrontations between living traditions.

2. The Bible comes first to people; afterwards they come to it. It becomes a book of and for the whole world (oikoumene). The task of teaching the Bible in an ecumenical perspective becomes one of inviting and encouraging students to make a pilgrimage to it and with it. The Bible becomes the critical element, the corrective framework of our ecumenical life and work. It is always important to bear in mind that Bible study was and is a foundation of the ecumenical movement in this century.

3. The Bible is itself a uniting factor, shared by all Christians. Across the barriers of many cultures and church traditions we are called to discover our unity in the one Bible. Biblical scholarship is, in this light, an instrument of Christian unity, and a necessary corrective to our one-sided perspectives. The Bible united the people of God in view of God's purpose, and it is the task of the biblical scholar to facilitate this

process. The work of Bible translation can and should be a cooperative ecumenical enterprise. As the message of the gospel is translated into other languages, it becomes possible to appreciate the unity of the Bible in the diversity of its expression in various cultural and linguistic frames of reference.

4. Any ecumenically-conscious approach to biblical scholarship must take into account the place of the Bible as but one sacred book among others in the several religious traditions. Within Christianity there is no clear Christian consensus on the nature of the authority of scripture, beyond the fact that all Christians view the Bible in some way as the word of God. It will be helpful to consider the place of the Judeo-Christian Bible among the other sacred texts and the scriptures of other religious traditions.

5. The exegetical question of how to understand the Bible is a central concern of biblical scholarship. In general there are at least three distinct ways of studying the Bible:

a) devotional-intuitive approach;
b) socio-experiential approach;
c) academic-critical approach.

Each approach has its uses and strengths, and it is essential to give attention to all three methods.

From an ecumenical perspective it is also essential to make students aware of the scholarly assumptions regarding the diversity of ancient historical contexts contained within the Bible. Here a discussion of these diversities within the context of the unity of the scriptures will shed light on the practical concerns of the ecumenical movement itself. [1]

6. The hermeneutical task is likewise a necessary component of teaching the Bible in ecumenical perspective. By means of hermeneutics the biblical scholar approaches the results of exegetical work in relation to the "here and now". A variety of contextual realities will help to determine which hermeneutic approach is appropriate for which local application and response, but helping students to appreciate the variety of possible approaches serves to liberate the study of the Bible from historical captivity, from transcendental religious and ethical norms, from dogmatic rigidity, and from methodological exclusivity, and lays a foundation for future ecumenical dialogue and encounter. Ecumenical teaching of the Bible is a process which suggests the liberation of peoples, the restructuring of the church as the people, and the creation of a new solidarity among peoples. For this reason, programmes in biblical education must not be limited strictly to the biblical materials *per se*, but must include a consideration of contemporary issues in order to develop an ecumenical perspective within different contexts. Such an effort may in fact lead to a kind of "ecumenical hermeneutic" which takes as its norm the solidarity and unity of the whole of humankind. More will be said of this concern in the next section of this paper.

Issues

Within the ecumenical movement today there are several major themes or issues which have direct impact on the teaching of the Bible in ecumenical perspective.

1. The contextual approach

If we understand that the Bible is the expression of faith by the peoples of the Old and New Testaments within their own particular historical contexts, we must also recognize the importance of teaching/learning the Bible within our own particular historical contexts. The assertion must be made that God speaks to every race and culture, and that the message communicated is adapted according to the situation of the hearer in each generation. Current socio-economic and political issues must be considered. Contemporary stories of suffering and oppression should be related not only to the stories of the Hebrews in Egypt and the *ochlos* in Palestine, but also to the biblical stories of Jesus who was/is the liberator of the poor, the oppressed, the alienated, the marginalized, the "sinners". All biblical interpretation is contextual.

2. *The topical approach*

The topical or thematic approach to the study of the Bible calls for the teaching and purposeful consideration of biblical themes such as creation, covenant, exodus, prophetic proclamations, salvation, Christ, kingdom of God, gospel, church, and so on. This method allows scholars to compare various confessional interpretations and emphases, and to discover convergences and consensus on the understanding of these respective themes.

3. *The trajectories approach*

A trajectory is a scheme of continuities that enables us to discern tendencies or emphases which tend to recur in scripture, and allows us to observe the influences which flow from one period of biblical history to another. In some ways the trajectory approach is similar to the topical approach, although the trajectories tend to be more abstract and philosophical than the topical subjects. For instance one might follow the trajectory of wisdom, or the royal trajectory, or the liberation trajectory. Much exciting work is being done in and for the ecumenical movement in this form of biblical research. Comparative studies of the royal trajectory and the liberation trajectory give a great deal of insight to the milieu of the biblical narrative, for example. The royal trajectory appears to have been fostered and valued among the urban elite, and tends to be socially conservative, with a primary valuing of stability. Its focus is on the glory and holiness of God's person, and it is institutionally geared to upholding that holiness. The liberation trajectory, by way of contrast, appears to have been fostered and valued among peasant communities, and tends to be socially revolutionary with a primary valuing of cultural transformation. Its focus is on the justice and righteousness of God's will. That the Bible contains and supports both trajectories is provocative material for ecumenical thinking.

4. *The feminist approach*

We can follow the lead of feminist scholars who have applied a hermeneutics of suspicion to the Bible, reading "between the lines" in search of evidence of the presence and involvement of the marginalized, and especially of women themselves. The strength of this approach is the enlistment of a broad variety of methodological tools drawn from several academic disciplines in the task of discerning and promoting the status of women in the Bible and the world.

5. *The approach of intra-biblical dialogue*

This approach to biblical study examines the instances when the Bible is in ecumenical dialogue with itself, i.e. when the New Testament texts comment critically upon the Old Testament texts. Other examples of intra-biblical ecumenical dialogue can be found in Acts 2, when on the day of Pentecost Peter interprets the prophecy of the second chapter of Joel, or when Peter's vision of the unclean creatures (Acts 10) causes him to reconsider the dietary restrictions imposed on the Jews by Leviticus (chapter 11). Yet another type of intra-biblical ecumenical dialogue is that which presents conversations between persons of different faiths and/or philosophies, such as Paul and Barnabas in their encounter with the Lycaonians in Acts 14, or Paul's discussion with the Greek philosophers in Acts 17. Many other examples are possible, but the implications of this kind of focus for the ecumenical movement should be obvious.

Tentative outline of course

I. Bible as living tradition
A. The invitation to Bible pilgrimage
    1) Historical issues and contexts
    2) Contemporary issues and parallels

B. Various approaches to the Bible
    1) Devotional-intuitive approach
    2) Socio-experiential approach
    3) Academic-critical approach

II. Biblical exegesis
A. Diversities of historical contexts within the Bible
B. The unity in diversity of scripture
C. Biblical authority
    1) In various Christian communities
    2) In the context of the sacred texts of other living faiths

III. Biblical hermeneutics
A. The contextual approach
B. The topical approach
C. The trajectories approach
D. The feminist approach
E. The intra-biblical ecumenical dialogue approach

IV. Biblical theologies
A. Towards a theology of unity
B. Coping with diversity
C. The norm of ecumenical solidarity

V. Uses of the Bible in the ecumenical movement
A. Bible study to enrich and inform
B. Liturgy and worship
C. Ecumenical translation of Bible

Conclusion

The Bible has many uses in the Christian community and beyond. It has been treated as a literary work, as a devotional guide, as an object of scholarly attention, as a liturgical resource, as an ideological-sociological phenomenon. But in Christian pastoral practice, that is in the preaching, teaching and worship of the church, it is used to illustrate, to persuade, to inspire and to call to action. Serious, lively, and informed biblical scholars have thus a significant role to play in making the Bible more readily accessible and understandable in the variety of contexts in which people use and study it.

For this reason, it is extremely valuable that these same biblical scholars should be trained in reading the Bible in ecumenical perspective. In the light of this ecumenical commitment, they can further the search for visible unity by their teaching and preaching, and can begin to build the community of solidarity and unity which the church is called to become.

Bibliography

Achtemeier, Paul, *An Introduction to the New Hermeneutic*, Philadelphia, Westminster Press, 1969.

Ariarajah, Wesley, *The Bible and People of Other Faiths*, Geneva, WCC, 1986.

Brueggemann, Walter, "Trajectories in Old Testament Literature and the Sociology of Ancient Israel", *JBL*, 98, 1980, p.162.

Buss, Martin, ed., *Encounter with the Text*, Philadelphia, Fortress Press, 1980.

Fiorenza, Elisabeth Schussler, *In Memory of Her: a Feminist Theological Reconstruction of Christian Origins*, New York, Crossroad, 1983.

Flesseman van Leer, Ellen, ed., "The Bible: its Authority and Interpretation in the Ecumenical Movement", *Faith and Order Paper No. 99*, Geneva, WCC, 1983.

Freire, Paulo, *Pedagogy of the Oppressed*, New York, Herder & Herder, 1970.

Gottwald, Norman F., *The Bible and Liberation: Political and Social Hermeneutics*, Maryknoll, Orbis, 1983.

Hineham, Dennis, *The Use and Abuse of the Bible: a Study of the Bible in an Age of Rapid Cultural Change*, London, 1976.

Mbiti, John S., *The Bible and Theology in African Christianity*, Oxford, Oxford University Press, 1986.

Ökumenisches Lernen, Kirchenamt der Evangelischen Kirche in Deutschland, Gutersloher Verlagshaus Gerd Mohn, 1985.

Weber, Hans-Reudi, *Experiments with Bible Study*, Geneva, WCC, 1983.

NOTE

[1] Cf. *Faith and Order Paper No. 99*, "The Bible: Its Authority and Interpretation in the Ecumenical Movement", ed. Ellen Flesseman-van Leer, Geneva, WCC, 1983.

14. Teaching Church History from an Ecumenical Perspective

Clarifications

Key terms such as *history, church history,* and *ecumenism* are often understood in various ways and need clarification so that we could discuss on the same wave-length or specify our different perceptions.

1. *History* is both the record and interpretation of the distant and immediate past. The notion of history as *res gestae* (things which happen) purveyed by Von Ranke has been found difficult to maintain because we are confronted with fragments of the past and, therefore, must *reconstruct* and interpret the fragments. All histories are written from interpretative perspectives.

2. *Church history* has been understood differently through the ages. At one point, church history was seen by some as an aspect of civilization history and coterminous with the rise and fall of civilizations. Others, mainly theologians, perceived church history as continuation of *salvation history (Heilsgeschichte)*. Still others treated the subject as *institutional history*; for them, church history would start when the missionary arrives and builds his first hut!

The perception taken here is that church history is much more. As T.V. Philip put the matter: "It is the history of a people's corporate response to the challenges of the gospel and their living and growing in constant dialogue with the religious and cultural situations in which they live."[1]

It is a people's history of their perception of God's saving grace in the midst of their struggles for survival. We understand the church to be the whole people of God and church history as the past of the whole people, the powerful as well as the marginalized.

3. This leads us to a clarification of the predicate of this view of church history, namely, *ecumenism*. We understand this to refer to God's creation of and lordship over the whole inhabited earth. It is a new understanding of what God has done in Jesus Christ, who invites us to a new and wider vision, learning and action. As perceived by Christians, ecumenism calls for a wider understanding of the church than is held at present, in the context of its mission in the contemporary world, of its relation to humankind as a whole. It calls for dialogue with other religions and spiritual traditions and incorporates the perspectives of the poor, of women, and of the oppressed. Viewed from below, ecumenism *is* a perspective of the world by the suffering, the poor, and the marginalized. It is a concern for the salvation of the whole creation.

The universal idea involved in this perception has throughout history been challenged by constricting, particularist views. In recent times, however, these constricting, narrow views have been rejected by the affirmations of the mandate to corporately express the Christian hope for the fullness of life.

Implications

The goal of church history

These clarifications carry a number of implications. The first relates to the goal of doing church history. The first task is to ask the simple question: *Why* do we write church history and for *whom*?

Church history from an ecumenical perspective endeavours to assist a community of believers to reflect on their past. Their past consists of the changes which have occurred in their cultural and economic lives and as a result of God's activities among them. It is a committed, purposeful interpretation designed to empower communities and individuals to gain a sense of their identity in their pilgrimage for the future. Church history also preserves a sense of continuity and tradition for future generations.

This perspective avoids an *elitist historiography* as well as many other biases which have characterized the writing of church history in the past. Elitist history focuses on climaxes, peak periods, certain classes of people such as kings, bishops, and prominent people and male leaders, to the neglect of certain others such as women, young people, children, indigenous communities, and the poor. Elitist history is written by the educated and powerful classes for their own consumption, legitimation and preservation of a certain sense of reality. Ecumenical church history must be holistic; it must paint the full profile of a community and focus on the fullness of God's creation.

The second bias is typified by *missionary historiography*, which is history written by missionaries and their protegés. Missionary historiography is propagandist and reflects the dominant ethnocentric ideologies of the metropoles and tends to diminish the contributions of native peoples in the spread of the gospel. The basic attitude to traditional cultures is often too judgmental to register the salient features and beauty of God's creation. Such historians call what God has created unclean. Besides, the objects of Christ's saving grace neither participate in writing their own histories nor feature in the pages. Many have died as unsung soldiers of Christ, bearing their unrecorded memories with them.

A third type which has bedevilled church history is *confessional* and *denominational historiography*. On the surface, it is salutary for each confessional group to tell its own story. Such histories constitute the data for reconstructing how people have responded to the gospel, the institutions which they built, and the doctrines which they affirmed. However, confessional histories perceive reality with a bias. They tend to extol their authenticity and achievements while denigrating the authenticity of others. They select certain facts of history to the neglect of others and, therefore, fail to be holistic. They destroy the unity of the church by building walls which separate.

A fourth bias, *nationalist historiography*, is, in some way, a reaction to both missionary and confessional historiographies. Self-awareness and the recovery of a sense of national identity have produced a nationalist historiography which is defensive and purportedly corrective of misconceptions. It seeks to recover ignored and despised data from the grassroots. There is little doubt that local studies are important. But nationalist histories wear their own blinders and are equally selective in the use of fragments of evidence. They also build their own walls which separate.

Writing history should be a process of self-discovery. There is a saying that "a person who does not know where the rain met him could not possibly know where he is going". Writing history from an ecumenical perspective should be a form of liberation — liberation from the narrowness of race, confession, ideology, nation, sex, and other forces which distort our perception of reality. It should also be a liberation from the burdens of the past. It is a means of building a strong, coherent band of pilgrims who know where they are coming from, their mission in the critical present, and their hope in the future.

Methodology

These assertions lead us ineluctably to the second question: *how* do we write church history from an ecumenical perspective? Our methodology should be predicated on certain principles, summarized as follows.

1. We must take a broad view of world history so as to eschew regional imbalances.

2. We must avoid confessional distortions and the emphases on certain confessions to the neglect of others. Church history should also study fringe movements and groups characterized as heretical. Confessional controversies and divisions should be taught from broader, comparative perspectives.

3. We must affirm the authenticity of the church history of each nation so that the church history of a country should be taught as a part of the total history of that country. The tendency to study the church history of some countries only as a part of missiology distorts.

4. We must do church history from an interdisciplinary perspective, so as to constantly refurbish the methodology.

5. Church history must be taught in such a way that the past comes alive: it should not be a mere chronicle of events; it should be relevant by bearing on the ecumenical issues and problems which we face today; and it should be experiential, involving teachers and students to experience the life of the church in different confessions and cultural situations.

Ecumenical perspective, however, does not diminish the importance of local communities. A man who wants to build a house must start with the foundation. A grassroots approach involves dialogue with the plurality of religious forms, a full profile of the community before the incursion of the Christian change-agent, and an assessment of the encounter and responses of the people. Church history is not what missionaries did or did not do, but how communities which had their living cultures responded to the gospel. It should not concentrate on the activities of clerics to the neglect of the contributions of the laity.

Various methods have been suggested, including the use of local church history committees, which ensure greater participation; the use of oral tradition; culture-area approaches which highlight how dominant cultural forms determined the reception of the gospel; and other social-science research methods.

A persistent problem in doing church history is the problem of periodization. An aspect of this problem is the hazard of imposing Western secular and ecclesiastical periodization upon the rest of the world. Periodization does not follow any hard-and-fast rules. It follows, rather, the contours of each nation's history and the presence of the gospel in its encounter with the cultures of the world.

Finally, a word must be said about the sources for doing church history. The teaching of church history should include teaching about the *sources* and methods of collecting data as well as the canons of interpretation. The *canons* are often referred to as *rules of evidence* which are designed to obviate distortions.

Broadly, there are primary sources, secondary sources, and plastic sources. Primary sources would include: (1) archival materials from government, missionaries, church records, diaries, obituary notices, tombstones, and archaeological data; (2) oral tradition — myths, folk-tales, proverbs, etc.; (3) oral history — contemporary recollections, interview reports, etc. Secondary sources would include written sources and interpretative materials. Plastic sources refer to fine and applied art objects.

Suggested themes for a curriculum on ecumenical church history

A.
1. Historiography
2. Definition of church history and ecumenical perspectives in doing church history
3. Methods of doing local church history
    a) Sources
    b) Field work techniques
    c) Oral tradition

B.
1. Christianity and society in the early church
    a) Church and state
    b) Church and culture
    c) Development of centres of Christianity
    d) Formulation of doctrines, liturgies, and ecclesiastical structures
    e) Ecumenical endeavours for reconciliation ministry
2. The church and society in the medieval period
    a) New religious movements
    b) The Great Schism
    c) Doctrinal controversies and challenge to Orthodoxy
    d) Popular piety
    e) A critical analysis of the crusade idea
    f) The Reformation: Protestant, Roman Catholic, and radical
    g) Religious liberty and religious toleration

C.
1. Cross-cultural mission in the six continents
    a) Through the sixteenth century
    b) Seventeenth and eighteenth centuries and the rise of denominations
    c) Nineteenth century and the Evangelical revival, missionary policy and ideology
2. Comparative analysis of church politics and liturgies
3. The church and the drums of war
4. Church and nationalism
5. Patterns of Christian presence in the six continents

D.
6. The church in the modern period: *domestication* of Christian values
    a) Church and education
    b) The church, power, and political values
    c) The church and social and economic order
7. The growth of the church in the six continents
    a) Indices of church growth, comparative statistical analysis of church growth
    b) The rise of new Christian movements, for example, independent churches in the third world
8. Current issues and concerns
    a) Church and movements of liberation
    b) Ecumenical movements: dialogue among churches and with other religions; church union movements; debate on indigenization, moratorium, etc.
    c) New perspectives on the mission and understanding of the church

It is assumed that these themes will be studied from the perspectives dealt with earlier. Moreover, certain themes run through the whole of church history.

Conclusion

To speak of church history in ecumenical perspective is to bring out our common history as "the history of how the universality of the gospel and the catholicity of the church are manifested in each age and in each situation" (T.V. Philip).

Bibliography

Baëta, Christian, ed., *Christianity in Tropical Africa*, London, Oxford University Press, 1968.

Brown, Colin, *Forty Years On: a History of the National Council of Churches in New Zealand, 1941-1981*, Christchurch, National Council, 1981.

Crow, Paul A. Jr., and William Jerry Boney, eds, *Church Union at Midpoint*, New York, Association Press, 1972.

Delumeau, Jean, ed., *Histoire vécue du peuple de Dieu*, 2 volumes, Toulouse, Privat, 1979.

Deschner, John, et al. eds., *Our Common History as Christians*, essays in honour of Albert C. Outler, New York, Oxford University Press, 1975.

Dessaux, Jacques-Elisée, *Vingt siècles d'histoire oecuménique*, Paris, Cerf, 1983. English translation: *Twenty Centuries of Ecumenism*, New York, Ramsey, Paulist Press, 1984.

Dussel, Enrique, *A History of the Church in Latin America. Vol. 5: Colonialism and Liberation, 1492-1979*, Grand Rapids, Eerdmans, 1981.

Ecumenical Initiatives in Eastern Africa, bibliography, AMECEA Research Department, Eldoret, Kenya, 1983, pp.102-106, J: Historical background.

Forman, Charles W., *The Island Churches of the South Pacific: Emergence in the 20th Century*, Maryknoll, Orbis, 1982 (American Society of Missiology Series, 5).

Geschichte der Ökumenischen Bewegung, Göttingen, Vandenhoeck & Ruprecht. I: 1517-1948, eds R. Rouse and St. Ch. Neill. 2 Bände, 1957-1958; II: 1948-1968, ed. Harold E. Fey. Deutsche Ausg., Günther Gassmann, 1974.

Harvey, Dorothy M., *...There is no End*, checklist of EACC-CCA publications and other ecumenical documents, 1948-1981, Toa Payoh, CCA, s.a. (cf. pp.47ff.: Related Asian Ecumenical Documents).

Hastings, Adrian, *Ecumenical Development in Africa*, AFER, Vol. VII, No. 2, p.113.

History of the Ecumenical Movement, London, SPCK. Vol. 1, 1518-1948, Ruth Rouse and Stephen C. Neill, eds, 1954; Vol. 2, 1948-1968, Harold E. Fey, ed., 1970.

Ökumenische Kirchengeschichte, eds Raymund Kottje and Bernd Moeller, Mainz: Grünewald/ München: Kaiser. 1: Alte Kirche und Ostkirche, 1970. 2: Mittelalter und Reformation, 1973. 3: Neuzeit, 1974.

Perumalil, H.C. and E.R. Hambye, eds, *Christianity in India: a History in Ecumenical Perspective*, Prakasam Publications, 1972.

Sanneh, Lamin, *West African Christianity: the Religious Impact*, London, C. Hurst & Co., 1983.

Schmidt, Dietrich and Ernst Wolf, eds, *Die Kirche in ihrer Geschichte: ein Handbuch*, Göttingen, Vandenhoeck & Ruprecht (Erscheint in Lieferungen ab 1962).

TEF Study Guide, London, SPCK. 5: Church History I: AD 29-500: the First Advance (John Foster), 1972. 8: Church History 2: AD 500-1500: Setback and Recovery (John Foster), 1974. 14: Church History 3: AD 1500-1800. Reformation, Rationalism, Revolution (Alan Thomson), 1976.

Vischer, Lukas, ed., *Ecumenical Association of Third World Theologians: Towards a History of the Church in the Third World*, papers and reports of a consultation on the issue of periodization..., 17-21 July 1983, Bern, Evang. Arbeitsstelle Ökumene Schweiz, 1985.

Vischer, Lukas, ed., *Church History in an Ecumenical Perspective*, papers and reports of an international ecumenical consultation, Basel, October 1981, Bern, Evang. Arbeitsstelle Ökumene Schweiz, 1982.

Weber, Hans-Ruedi, *Asia and the Ecumenical Movement*, 1895-1961, London, SCM, 1966.

NOTE

[1]*Christianity in India*, p.300.

15. Teaching Systematic Theology in an Ecumenical Perspective

The task of systematic theology

1. We would like to use two phrases to summarize the task of systematic theology: (1) as Christians we are called to give an account of the hope that is within us (1 Pet. 3:15); (2) because the faith that we have is a faith that responds to life and experience, systematic theology must always be "faith seeking understanding" (*fides quaerens intellectum*). As *theology*, then, systematics is a reflective act, responsive both to revelation and to concrete experience. As a discipline, systematic theology must also be in constant dialogue with, on the one hand, the mission of the church, and, on the other hand, the praxis of the church.

2. As *systematic*, theology must be viewed as the coherent relationship of the main themes of Christian doctrine as they inform and influence each other. There is no sense in which systematic theology can be viewed as a *closed* system. Rather, system must be understood, in this context, in "organic" terms, as something open to revision, revisable, with an emphasis on the dialogical nature of education. It, like the church, must live under the principle of *semper reformandum*.

3. This is so partly because of the sources upon which a truly ecumenical systematic theology must draw. Not only the traditional sources for theology (the Bible, philosophical thinking, *dogmengeschichte*, and the doxological life of the church — its liturgical traditions, patterns and traditions of spirituality and devotion), but also and above all the lives and struggles of its people. This latter is not meant primarily to be the object of theological enquiry, but as a *locus* of primary theological reflection. This means, too, that systematic theology must have a broad epistemological base, with attention to, e.g., understanding to be gained from the sociology of knowledge and "bodily epistemology" as developed in feminist contexts.

4. A point of importance for doing an ecumenical systematic theology comes from the common task we have as Christians to give an account of our hope: a common identity can emerge through the need to confess Christ in a variety of contexts. So-called "contextual theologies", therefore, have a major role to play in contemporary systematic theology, especially in an ecumenical perspective. As the people and churches of our one global community struggle to make the gospel and the church's mission live in their own context, so all of our theological understandings can be enriched by each other's experience. "Contextual theology", then, is shared theological reflection; a sharing of theology in response to life.

5. An ecumenical systematic theology, then, must be inclusive of inductive and deductive methods, taking full account of theological reflection arising out of concrete social, historical, political and cultural situations. As *ecumenical*, this must lead to a broader understanding of our common confession of Christ, and to a genuine listening to and learning from each other. An ecumenical systematic theology, therefore, will also be characteristically corporate and engaged.

The obstacles and challenges to an ecumenical perspective in systematic theology

6. By their very nature, the obstacles that stand in the way of having an ecumenical perspective in systematic theology are also some of the challenges. Entrenched denominationalism, for instance, stands as a real obstacle to an ecumenical perspective. But it also stands as a challenge: an ecumenical perspective is a challenge to denominations to be "liberated" from an enslavement to a tyrannous theology (and the tyrannous aspects of denominational power, resources, culture and so on), and to drink from the ever-flowing fountain of our common confession of Christ, the challenge to be enriched theologically.

7. The divorce, too, between theology and life can stand in the way of ecumenical systematics. This is also the challenge to theology to be engaged, to search the contexts of theologies for the insights that arise from a living Christian faith.

8. Another obstacle to an ecumenical perspective can come from the divorce of theology from the mission of the church. Theology is, but is not only, an academic discipline, nor is it the monopoly of professional theologians. It is also reflection by the whole people of God on an encounter with the risen Christ, and on the experience of trying to be the church in and for the world.

9. The obstacles and challenges to an ecumenical perspective in systematic theology are many. Our point here in mentioning some of them is to encourage each confession and each theologian to examine their own self-understanding to uncover those ways in which they might be inhibiting an ecumenical perspective.

Some general principles for teaching systematic theology in an ecumenical perspective

10. The following are points that we feel should guide in the teaching of systematic theology in an ecumenical perspective:

a) In teaching systematic theology in an ecumenical perspective one must consciously and deliberately draw on theological resources that go beyond confessional, cultural, social and political boundaries. This should be done in such a way that one does not lose one's confessional identity, but enlarges understanding and vision.

b) In teaching systematic theology in an ecumenical perspective, one must be mindful of the questions and challenges that arise out of the contexts in which Christian faith is lived. Because of its dialogical nature an ecumenical systematic theology must pay attention to both kerygmatic and existential questions, questions arising from the human predicament and from the testing of faith in context. It must also be open to and aware of being questioned by God.

c) An ecumenical teaching of systematic theology must also seek criteria in judging itself, expecially those criteria that lead towards unity and away from the natural human tendency to inward-looking parochialism. This is not so much an effort to avoid conflict or argument, but to seek through conflict and argument those things that make for and facilitate unity.

d) An ecumenical systematic theology will also seek to be true to its own nature as an *integrating* discipline. It will seek to incorporate the fruits of other theological disciplines (biblical studies, church history, ethics) into its own work. It must therefore be a listening, interpreting and synthesizing discipline.

e) The teaching of an ecumenical systematic theology must also be doxological in character, done within the framework of praise and celebration and prayer. Because of the nature of an ecumenical systematic theology (as faith seeking understanding), doing theology cannot be viewed as an end in itself; it comes from praise and leads to praise and must be liberated from taking itself too seriously. As an aspect of praise it is meant to be enjoyed!

f) An important principle in teaching systematic theology in an ecumenical perspective has to do with what might be called the life-style of the theologian: an ecumenical perspective is as much caught as taught. The stories of holy women and men, from both the ancient and contemporary history of the church, form not only an important resource for theology, but also an important link between the discipline of systematic theology and the spirituality and praxis of the church. It is often from the stories of holy women and men that we ourselves can learn to be holy.

An introduction to an ecumenical systematic theology

The preceding parts of this report are of primary importance and of a higher priority than the following "basic course outline" for an introduction to an ecumenical systematic theology. Those teaching already existing courses are asked to examine and adjust their courses in the light of these principles. It is, therefore, imperative that this outline is read in the light of the principles outlined above. Starting with the outline before reading the principles will only lead to confusion.

Those in the process of creating courses in systematic theology are encouraged *not* simply to follow the suggested course as it stands, but to adapt, rearrange, delete and add to it as their own context demands. For instance, in certain contexts one might wish to begin from the Person and work of the Holy Spirit; in others it might be deemed more appropriate to begin with humanity and the human struggle.

BASIC COURSE OUTLINE

I.   Introduction
II. The main themes of Christian theology
     God
     Jesus/Christ
     The Person and work of the Holy Spirit
     Salvation
     Humanity
     The world
     The future
     Church and ministry
III. Final unit: theology and church

Note concerning this course outline:

1. The nature of this course is meant to be *introductory*, and presumes that more detailed work on any number of points may take place later.

2. "Introductions" to various units or sections of units are meant to allow the person using the outline to make the unit or section specific to his or her own context. This is also true of sections which are "suggestive" (rather than "prescriptive") of content (e.g., the unit on God, section D, number 3; section E, number 2; the unit on humanity, section C; the unit on the future, section C, etc.).

UNIT OUTLINES

I. Introduction: the kingdom of God as the foundation of systematic theology

A. Introduction
B. The kingdom of God in the preaching of Jesus
C. The kingdom of God and the main themes of Christian theology
D. Systematic theology and other intellectual disciplines

II. The main themes of Christian theology

God
A. Introduction
   1) Language
   2) Context
B. The God of Israel
   1) Introduction
   2) God and the covenant with Israel
   3) The prophets
C. "The God and the Father of our Lord Jesus Christ"
D. The development of our understanding of God
   1) Post-apostolic Christianity
   2) The Triune God
   3) Post-patristic Christianity
E. Contemporary understandings of God
   1) Introduction
   2) The twentieth century

Jesus/Christ
A. Introduction: what is Christology? Christology and soteriology
B. Biblical foundations
C. Historical/theological development of Christology
   1) Introduction
   2) Patristic Christology
   3) The Chalcedonian definition (AD 451)
D. Some modern Christologies

The person and work of the Holy Spirit
A. Introduction
B. God as Spirit
   1) Biblical foundations

    2) Patristic development
    3) Contemporary understandings
C. The Spirit in/and the church
    1) "Lord and giver of life"
    2) Charismatic renewal
D. The Spirit in/and the world

Humanity
A. Introduction
B. "What is man that you are mindful of him" (Ps. 8)
    1) Biblical anthropology
    2) Patristic anthropology
    3) Other culturally specific anthropologies
C. Some modern Christian anthropologies

The world
A. Introduction
    1) Guiding principles
    2) The world in the New Testament
B. Mission/culture
    1) Issues of the gospel and development
C. Ethics/culture
    1) Systematic theology as ethics
    2) Culture and context

The future
A. Introduction: the future as God's future
B. The future in the past
    1) General
    2) The "four last things"
       a) Resurrection
       b) Judgment/heaven and hell
C. The future in the present: *After Death: Life in God*: a "process theology" view

Church and ministry
A. Introduction
B. Ministers of the kingdom
    1) Biblical perspective
    2) Communities of the kingdom
    3) From kingdom to church
    4) Kinds of ministry
C. Word and sacrament
D. Ministers of the church
    1) Lima/BEM
    2) Bilateral convergences
    3) Conclusions

III. Theology and church
A. Introduction
B. "Practical theology"
    1) The priestly role of theology: theology as the servant of the church
    2) Theology as prophet to the church
    3) "Doing theology": the contexts of primary theological reflection
C. Ecumenical theology/ecumenical praxis

Bibliography

Because the course outlined here is meant to be adaptable to many contexts we have held back from producing too specific a bibliography: this would have limited its usefulness. Therefore we would like to draw attention to the other bibliographies contained in this volume, and we mention here only a few books that should be of help in finding material which can be used in this course.

Basdekis, A. *et al.*, Hrsg, *Ökumene Lexikon*, Kirchen, Religionen, Bewegungen, Frankfurt AM, Verlag Otto Lembeck, Verlag Josef Knecht, 1983.

Beffa, P., *et al.* eds, *Index to the WCC's Official Statements and Reports*, Geneva, WCC, 1978.

van der Bent, A.J., *A Guide to Essential Ecumenical Reading*, Geneva, WCC, 1984.

van der Bent, A.J., *Six Hundred Ecumenical Consultations 1948-1982*, Geneva, WCC, 1983.

Fouilloux, E., *Les catholiques et l'unité chrétiènne du XIXe au XXe siècle*, Paris, Le Centurion, 1982.

International Ecumenical Bibliography (four languages), München, Chr. Kaiser Verlag, Mainz, Matthias-Grünewald-Verlag, 1963-.

Littell, F.H. and H.H. Walz Hrsg, *Weltkirchenlexikon*, Stuttgart, Kreuz-Verlag, 1960.

Meyer, H. and L. Vischer eds, *Growth in Agreement*, Geneva, WCC, 1984, reports and agreed statements of ecumenical conversations on a world level.

Morgan, R., *Sisterhood is Global*, New York, Anchor Books, 1984, the international women's movement anthology.

SOME JOURNALS
WCC, *The Ecumenical Review*.
T. & T. Clark, *Concilium*.
Temple University, *Journal of Ecumenical Studies*.
Chr. Kaiser Verlag, *Verkündigung und Forschung* (all issues, but see especially volume 1/1985 for bibliographies of important so-called "contextual" and regional theologies).

16. The Search for Unity in an Interfaith Setting

Introduction

A. The aims of teaching this subject are:

1) To bring an awareness that interfaith relations form an essential part of the ecumenical perspective for the Christian church in today's world.

2) To explore the implication of the Christian concern for the unity of the human community which is made up of vast numbers of persons belonging to other faiths.

3) To clarify the Christian self-understanding and the claim of the church in the light of the interfaith dialogue and religious pluralism.

4) To motivate students for increased interest in the faiths of their neighbours and promote involvement in issues of common concern for society and the world.

5) To discover new theological insights in the context of interfaith dialogue.

B. The rapid shrinking of our global villages into a nearer neighbourhood, the increasing presence of religious pluralism in all societies, the missionary challenge of other faiths, the growing menace of religious disharmony in many parts of the world, the biblical imperative of faithfulness to the gospel both in service and witness to our neighbours — all these and many more factors summon us to take interfaith relations as an essential part of the ecumenical perspective that we want to encourage in our churches.

C. The new situation of religious pluralism often brings new challenges and opportunities.

1) Christians have often studied other faiths from an apologetic and missionary motivation. Today we are becoming more aware of how interfaith dialogue opens us to the spirituality of other faiths and helps us both to appreciate and learn from them, so leading to a change of attitude and greater humility, repentance and readiness. For example, we must reject the attitude which regards the study of other faiths as a purely academic exercise, or a means of establishing the superiority of the Christian faith.

2) Interfaith dialogue clarifies the Christian self-understanding both in religiously plural and in secular settings. Interaction with other faiths enables the church to evaluate realistically her claims and contributions. Theologians should be

challenged to rethink expositions of traditional theological formulations such as those on Christology, the doctrine of salvation, the Trinity, etc., seeking a fresh understanding in the light of interfaith dialogue and religious pluralism. Interfaith dialogue, as a process in which Christians witness to their faith, and are prepared also to listen attentively to the witness of others, serves as a catalyst in the renewal of the church, helping her to sharpen her understanding of mission and witness.

3) Interfaith dialogue provides the opportunity to study the common issues that cut across society and to combine the resources of various faiths to build a better world. Women, for example, would be enabled to study the common issues affecting them and to build a community of solidarity across religious barriers, contributing to women's perspective in theology. The oppressed and marginalized in society would be enabled to take common action for their liberation motivated by the resources and insights of their own faith, enriched and corrected by others. Interfaith dialogue thus helps to bring together Christians and people of other faith communities for united action for social transformation.

Methodological considerations

A1)The Christian church shares with the human community a common heritage and wishes to share a distinctive message with them. It needs therefore to theologically reflect upon the nature of the community Christians seek, together with others, as it lives among others as a community of service and witness, without disturbing their faith or compromising their commitment to God in Christ.

2) Justice, peace and the integrity of creation have become a global concern which can be promoted through greater understanding and dialogue.

3) Christians get involved in such dialogue because of the message of reconciliation and promise of hope given in Christ. It is in obedience to the biblical vision of the eschatological gathering of all peoples that they are impelled to take this perspective seriously.

4) The interfaith perspective is not just one additional element in the teaching of ecumenics. It has to penetrate and interact within the total teaching of the theological curriculum and illumine the treatment of all subjects.

5) The setting of religious pluralism is not seen as a theological threat or problem, but a challenge and an opportunity to explore deeper into the theological and missionary task of the church.

B. Some learning/teaching suggestions

1) Wherever possible, teaching of other faiths must be by adherents of those faiths themselves, so that they may be allowed to "define" their own faith, bring its perspectives as a living faith, and emphatically interpret it.

2) Exposure to prayer and worship, festivals and celebrations, symbols and sites, with the assistance of practising members of the faith, is desirable. Experiencing the spirituality of other faiths is an integral part of learning about other faiths.

3) Case studies on religious harmony or communal strife is a useful way of understanding the political and cultural factors related to religious faith and the theological convictions and religious sentiments of people.

4) Reading selected texts from the scriptures and thus going directly to original sources should be encouraged; it will also raise the issue of authority and interpretation of scriptures in each faith.

5) Theological learning in an interfaith milieu happens best when it is grounded in dialogical practice, in the context of living in community with others, participating in everyday social life of the society. Ecumenical perspective demands existential participation.

An outline of the course

A. Ecumenism
  1) Perspectives in ecumenism (*oikoumene*, interchurch, interfaith)
  2) Models in ecumenism (e.g. exclusive, inclusive, pluralist)
  3) Historical developments in ecumenical thinking
  4) Ecumenism in the light of world economy, racism, sexism, politics and pluralism

B. Faiths encountering each other
  1) Why study other faiths?
  2) Historical review (selected case studies from around the world: missionary origins, church growth, inculturation, etc.)
  3) Developments in mutual attitudes of Christians and adherents of other faiths. Field-work through visits, etc. to be included
  4) Development of indigenous theology
  5) New forms of spirituality, new religious movements and their implications
  6) Religious fundamentalism, militant trends and their implications

C. Dialogue
1. *Practice and theory of dialogue*
  a) Historical review of modern interfaith dialogue
  b) Types: discursive, secular, interior, existential
  c) Some leading ideas: Christian presence; the hidden Christ; anonymous Christians; shared spirituality; cosmic covenant; religious pluralism; common humanity
  d) Ecclesiological issues in the light of interfaith dialogue
2. *A study of recent documents on dialogue*
  a) Vatican II: *Lumen Gentium, Ad Gentes, Nostra Aetate*
  b) WCC: *Guidelines on Dialogue; Mission and Evangelism: an Ecumenical Affirmation*
  c) Joint Working Group: *Common Witness*
  d) *The Lausanne Covenant*
3. *Towards new dimensions in the theology of dialogue*
  a) Biblical basis
  b) Salvation: limited or universal?
  c) Mission
  d) Syncretism
  e) Theology of religions

Suggested basic reading

Ariarajah, Wesley, *The Bible and People of Other Faiths*, Geneva, WCC, 1985.

Costas, Orlando, *Christ Outside the Gate: Mission Beyond Christendom*, Orbis, 1982.

Cracknell, Kenneth, *Theology on Full Alert*, London, British Council of Churches.

Cragg, Kenneth, *The Christian and Other Religions: the Measure of Christ*, London, Mowbray, 1977.

Hick, John, *God and the Universe of Faiths*, Macmillan, 1973.

Hillman, E., *The Wider Ecumenism*, Burns Oates, 1968.

Samartha, S.J. ed., *Living Faiths and the Ecumenical Movement*, Geneva, WCC, 1971.

Song, C.S., *Third Eye Theology*, New York, Orbis, 1979.

17. Social Ethics in an Ecumenical Perspective

Guidelines

A. The aims of teaching social ethics in an ecumenical perspective are:

1) To provide a sound basis for social ethics rooted in biblical and theological awareness in order to set questions of social ethics in an ecumenical context and evaluate different perspectives in this light.

2) To establish an ecclesiological awareness about what implications social questions have not only for the renewal of humankind but also for the unity of the church.

3) To provide opportunities for students to examine selected ethical issues of regional and global significance.

4) To promote involvement in social action for change in an ecumenical context, and reflection on the ethical implications of such involvement.

B. Focusing on the ecclesiological significance of an ecumenical social ethics, we need to emphasize that the ecumenical dimension of social ethics is deeply rooted in our confession of faith and in the sacramental life of the church. An ecumenical social ethics is an essential element of a church which understands itself as a *mystery and a prophetic sign for the world*. This concept of the church implies for the understanding of social ethics:

1) That the presence of Christ in the *mystery* of his church is not without his presence and solidarity with the poor and marginalized, because in Christ, God became poor and shared life with the poor and oppressed. Commitment for justice and peace therefore belongs to the very essence of the church.

2) That the church is not an end in itself, but is sent into the world as a sign, as an instrument for the fullfilling of God's kingdom. The underlying vision, related to the concrete mission of the church in the world, is *Shalom*, God's promise and gift of new creation in Christ.

3) That the unity of the church cannot be separated from the renewal of humankind, not only because divisions according to class, sex, race and poverty run through the diverse confessions and cross their boundaries, but mainly because any interconfessional unity without prior solidarity with the poor means to be out of touch with historical reality. A special contribution of social ethics for the direction of the ecumenical movement as a whole can be seen in the search for "a rele-

vant form of unity (which) includes the supreme care for the marginal"
(P. Crow).

Methodological considerations

For developing a course on ecumenical social ethics we offer some basic
methodological considerations and suggestions for teaching/learning.

A. Basic methodological considerations

1) The transforming power of Christ works both in individual lives and in wider
   communities. Therefore change in personal lives and change of social structures
   belong together and should be kept together in ecumenical social ethics.
2) Ecumenism is concerned with the witness of the whole church in the whole world.
   Therefore the discernment of God's redeeming action in and for the world includes
   an openness and awareness of problems of justice, peace and the integrity of
   creation in other parts of the world and a sensitivity towards acts of witness and
   ethical positions of other churches, denominations and confessions.
3) Christians must understand the world and its powers using critically tools available
   from the various social sciences and ideologies. The ecumenical encounter,
   therefore, includes the analysis of ideologies confronting each other and the search
   for truth with an open and critical mind.
4) Ecumenical social ethics will not accept uncritically any social analysis or ideology
   but will place them in the context of a biblical-theological search for the work of
   God in the world.
5) Ecumenical ethics is concerned over the repentance and renewal of the church in
   its mission to the world as witness to the judgment and promise of God for all
   people. It therefore includes a self-critical dimension with regard to the church and
   its witness.
6) Ecumenical ethics presupposes and reinforces the involvement of Christians in
   social service and action in the world. Learning through theological reflection,
   therefore, has to critically interact with practical commitment and involvement as
   an integral part of that process.

B. Some learning/teaching suggestions

1) It may be helpful to stimulate thought by beginning the course with a challenge to
   the Christian standpoint from some other religion or ideology, then bringing that
   perspective into dialogue with Christian thought. The same method can be used to
   present an alternative Christian view with which the students are not familiar.
   During a course it is often useful to bring into the classroom/learning situation
   representatives of differing perspectives on the issue discussed, whether Christian
   or others.
2) Another approach might be to involve students in some social ministry in their
   local situations, leading them through analysis of the problems of their own
   community to broader issues of stewardship, justice and peace. The interaction of
   local economic conditions with the world economy or with national policy is an
   obvious example. The relation of local politics to national policy and international
   alliances or conflicts is another. In any case students should be placed in or bring
   with them practical experience which forces them to struggle with ethical issues

that require ecumenical reflection. They should be asked to engage in this reflection in papers and in group discussion.

3) Any social ethics course should provide plenty of opportunity for group interaction. Panel discussions, debates, case studies, open-ended stories, simulation games, and common reflection on selected news reports could all be means of stimulating this interaction and of illuminating the problems at issue.

4) Whatever approach is used, on a level appropriate to the educational background and practical experience of the students, the interaction between present social conditions and biblical situations is critical for theological reflection. The world of the Bible, where God dealt with God's people and came to dwell on earth in Jesus Christ, illumines the work of God in the contemporary world. The object of any course in Christian social ethics is to discern how and where this work takes place in today's world.

A tentative course outline

A. Foreword

The dangers in proposing a course to be taught throughout the world are obvious. In discerning the judgment and promise of God in human society especially, the actual conditions in a given place and time must be a primary object of study. These conditions vary greatly from one part of the world to another. Nevertheless we believe that there are central problems of our time, of over-riding urgency and importance. The ecumenical movement, through the World Council of Churches and other worldwide Christian movements and associations, has played a significant role in this century in defining these problems and exploring the resources of the faith for dealing with them. It is this living contemporary history of the church ecumenical on which we draw in the outline and bibliography which follow. They should be adapted to local conditions. In many cases regional and national ecumenical literature is available to supplement what is suggested here. Often other social problems than those in the outline will be critical. But in so far as the ecumenical movement among Christians throughout the world has been faithful in its discernment, the issues we raise here are important for the church everywhere.

B. Suggested course outline

1. Theological foundations of Christian social ethics
   a) God's promise and judgment for the world in biblical tradition
   b) God's power and powers in the world
   c) The eschatological vision of the kingdom and the ethical goals of justice and peace
   d) Demands of the gospel, Christian responsibility and ethical compromise
2. World mission in social dimension
   a) The shape of the church and its social commitment
      — What forms of the church can be called missionary in the world today?
   b) Evangelism and social witness and action
      — What kind of social witness is demanded from Christians in different contexts?

    c) Interfaith dialogue and social action
- — How should Christians interact with persons of other faiths and ideologies on questions of peace, justice and the integrity of creation?

    d) Social changes and the signs of the kingdom
- — How can social changes be interpreted as signs of the coming kingdom?

3. Economics, technology and politics
   a) The promise and threat of technological development for the quality of human life
   b) Economic justice and economic power (Christian evaluation of socialism and free market ideology)
   c) Socio-economic and political problems of poverty
   d) Human rights, civil and economic
4. Racial justice and community
   a) The social and personal (local) essence of racism and racist structures
   b) Biblical and theological understanding of the ecumenical community of races; racism and the *status confessionis* of the church
   c) Church action against racism
   d) Injustice related to caste, ethnic minorities, etc.
5. Women and men in the church
   a) Changes in the relation between women and men
   b) Biblical interpretation and reinterpretation of the role of women and men in church and society
   c) Participation of women in the church's ministries, ordination of women, church leadership
6. The search for peace
   a) Christian pacifism and the theory of the just war
   b) Non-violence and the Christian participation in liberation and resistance movements
   c) The question of nuclear disarmament
   d) Christian peace-making and ecumenical expressions for peace
   e) Conflict and peace-making in the given region in church and society
7. Integrity of creation
   a) Relation between humanity and non-human creation
   b) The role of scientific investigation and technological development with regard to nature
   c) The problems and dangers of bio-engineering
   d) The task of the protection of the sustainability of the earth and the rights of future generations to enjoy the earth's fruits
8. The place of the disabled in human society
   a) Understanding the varieties of disabilities and forms of care and community support
   b) The role of the disabled in human community
   c) The rights of the disabled in society
9. Pastoral ministry informed by ecumenical social ethics
   a) Contextual issues for congregations
   b) Areas for joint action for churches
   c) Proclaiming God's justice through preaching and Bible study

Suggested basic reading

Abrecht, P. and Ninan Koshy eds, *Before It's Too Late: the Challenge of Nuclear Disarmament*, Geneva, WCC, 1983.

Abrecht, P., *The Churches and Rapid Social Change London*, London, SCM Press, 1961.

Abrecht, P. ed., *Faith and Science in an Unjust World*, report of the WCC's conference on "Faith, Science and the Future", Geneva, WCC, 1980.

Bennett, John C. ed., *Christian Social Ethics in a Changing World*, New York, Association Press, London, SCM, 1966.

Christians in the Technical and Social Revolutions of Our Time, report, World Conference on Church and Society, Geneva, 1966. Geneva, WCC, 1967.

Man's Disorder and God's Design, the Amsterdam Assembly Series 5 Vols. London, SCM Press, 1948.

The Pastoral Contribution of the Church in the Modern World (Lumen Gentium), Vatican II.

Preston, Ronald, *Church and Society in the Late Twentieth Century*, London, SCM Press, 1984.

de Santa Ana, Julio ed., *Towards a Church of the Poor*, Geneva, WCC, 1979.

The Uppsala Report 1968, Geneva, WCC, 1968.

Appendices

Appendix 1

To Seminaries, Divinity Schools and Faculties of Theology

Some Questions on Teaching Theology Ecumenically

A. Composition of staff and students

1. How is the faculty composed confessionally? How far do the given ecclesial accountabilities influence the direction and content of the programmes?
2. Are denominations other than those constitutionally linked with the school represented on the staff and are there opportunities to teach theology in inter-denominational dialogue?
3. What experiences do you have in teaching courses ecumenically and undertaking programmes that foster ecumenical encounter and dialogue?
4. What is the composition of the student community with regard to the variety of confessions, cultures and political situations present in your context?

B. Ecumenical goals

5. Is teaching theology in an ecumenical perspective one of your agreed purposes? If not, what are the factors that prevent this?
6. Are there programmes of cooperation with faculties, students and others of other confessional, cultural and political backgrounds?
7. Does your programme have partnership relations with institutions in other parts of the world?
8. Is there a department or chair or courses offered on ecumenics, mission and interfaith dialogue?

C. Teaching methodology

9. Do you offer interdisciplinary seminars related to ecumenical themes?
10. How many courses related to ecumenics are required/optional?
11. Are courses related to issues of justice, peace and the integrity of creation offered in your programme? Would "option for the poor" be an accepted perspective in your teaching and work?
12. Have any innovative ways of doing theology been attempted in your school? Are there programmes of involvement in local congregations and the community at large? Are these seen as an integral part of learning and teaching?
13. What is the role of students in deciding the content, method and style in the learning process?

D. Ecumenical cooperation

14. What are some of the obstacles and hindrances of greater ecumenical cooperation in your work?
15. Where do you see future possibilities in the development of the faculty and its ecumenical cooperation where ecumenical perspectives can be strengthened or included anew?
16. Are there areas where the Association of Theological Schools or the Programme on Theological Education of the World Council of Churches can be of assistance? What suggestions do you have towards these bodies in the area of promoting ecumenical perspectives and cooperation in theological education?

Appendix 2

List of Participants

Assad, Dr Maurice (Coptic Orthodox), Associate General Secretary, Middle East Council of Churches, El Max Street 2, Heliopolis, Cairo, Egypt

Arles, Mr Siga (Church of South India), Lecturer, South India Biblical Seminary, P.O. Box 20, Bangarapet 563114, Karnataka, India

Basile, Prof. Francesco (Roman Catholic), Priest/Lecturer, Contrada Guardia, 98010 S. Agata-Messina, Italy

Büchner, Dr Friedrich (Evangelical Lutheran), Pastor, Karolinenstr. 8, 5900 Eisenach, German Democratic Republic

Crawford, Rev. Janet (Anglican), Lecturer, St John's College, 202 St John's Road, Auckland 5, New Zealand

Crow, Dr Paul Jr (Disciples), President, Council of Christian Unity, Disciples of Christ, P.O.Box 1986, Indianapolis, IN 46206, USA

Dominguez, Ms Elizabeth (United Church of Christ), Lecturer, Union Theological Seminary, Dasmarinas, Cavite, Philippines

Draper, Dr Jonathan (Anglican), Lecturer, 19 High Street, Cuddesdon, Oxford, UK (USA)*

Falconer, Rev. Alan D. (Reformed), Lecturer, Irish School of Ecumenics, 20 Pembroke Park, Dublin 4, Ireland (UK)

Hall, Dr Mary (Roman Catholic), Lecturer/Director, Selly Oak Colleges, Bristol Road, Selly Oak, Birmingham B29 62Q, UK (Ireland)

Han, Mr June Shick (Presbyterian), Director of Planning, 222-64 Sangdong-Dong, Dong-daemun-ku, Seoul, Korea

Harrison, Ms Patricia (Presbyterian), Lecturer, 11 Garibaldi Street, Armidale, NSW 2350, Australia

Herche, Rev. Martin (Evangelical), Pastor, Kirchplatz 11, 5504 Heringen, German Democratic Republic

Kalu, Dr Ogbu U. (Presbyterian), Lecturer, University of Nigeria, Nsukka, Anambra State, Nigeria

Koukoura, Dr Dimitra (Orthodox), Lecturer, 37 Vas Konstantinon Avenue, 54622 Thessaloniki, Greece

Kwasi, Mr Ugira (Church of Christ in Zaire), Student, 53 rue des Glands, 1190 Brussels, Belgium (Zaire)

---

* Country of origin appears in brackets.

Lapointe, Fr Eugene (Roman Catholic), Lecturer, St Augustine's Seminary, P.O. Box 8, Roma 180, Lesotho (Canada)

Lee, Dr Ms Sung Hee (Presbyterian), Lecturer, Keimyung University, 634 Taegu, Korea

Mbiti, Dr John (Anglican), Pastor and Professor, Einschlagweg 11, 3400 Burgdorf, Switzerland

Merentek-Abram, Ms Sientje (Evangelical), Pastor/Educator, Fakultas Theologia UKIT, Tomohon, Sulut, Indonesia

Myint, Ms Sann Sann (Baptist), Youth Officer, No. 9, 49th Street, East Rangoon P.O., Rangoon, Burma

Nxumalo, Fr Jabulani (Roman Catholic), Priest/Lecturer, Casa Generalizia, C.P. 9061, 0010 Rome-Aurelio, Italy (South Africa)

Philip, Dr T.V. (Mar Thoma), Lecturer, 73 Kirwan Street, Keperra, Queensland 4054, Australia (India)

Phiri, Ms Isabel (Assemblies of God), Lecturer, Chancellor College, Box 280, Zomba, Malawi

Porcile-Santiso, Ms Maria (Roman Catholic), Bible translator/Teacher/Theologian, Av. Luis Ponce 1563/67, Montevideo, Uruguay

Richey, Dr Russell (United Methodist), Lecturer, The Divinity School, Duke University, Durham, NC 27706, USA

Rutiba, Rev. Eustace (Anglican), Associate Professor, Makerere University, P.O. Box 7062, Kampala, Uganda

Sanders, Ms Cheryl (Church of God), Lecturer, 7704 Morningside Drive N.W., Washington DC 20012, USA

Sandidge, Dr Jerry (Assemblies of God), Lecturer, Oral Roberts University, School of Theology and Mission, 7777 So. Lewis, Tulsa, OK 74171, USA

Sauca, Mr Ioan (Orthodox), Student, The Triangle, Block 4, Unit 33, Prittchatts Road, Birmingham B15, UK (Romania)

Schmidt, Dr Jean (United Methodist), Lecturer, The Iliff School of Theology, 2201 S. University Blvd, Denver, CO 80210, USA

Sekimoto, Rev (Anglican), Dean, 2-23-1 Mihara Naha, St Peter and St Paul's Cathedral, Okinawa, Japan 902

Smolik, Dr Josef (Brethren), Lecturer, Belgicka 22, Prague 2, Czechoslovakia

Spindler, Dr Marc (Reformed), Lecturer/Director, van Diepenburchstraat 25, 2597 PR The Hague, Netherlands

Suh, Dr David Kwang-sun (Presbyterian), Lecturer, 126-22 Daeshin-Dong, Suhdaemoon-ku, Seoul 120, Korea

Tuwere, Rev. Ilaitia S. (Methodist), Pastor, Pacific Theological College, P.O. Box 388, Suva, Fiji

Velasques, Dr Procoro (Methodist), Lecturer, C.P. 5002, 09720 San Bernardo do Campo, S/P Brazil

Wahba, Rev. Wafeek (Presbyterian), Evangelical Theological Seminary, 8 Sekah El Bedah, Abbasiah, Cairo, Egypt

Werner, Mr Dietrich (Evangelical Lutheran), Assistant Pastor, Evang. Studienwerk, Hans Villigst, 5840 Schwerte 5, Federal Republic of Germany

West, Dr Charles (Presbyterian), Lecturer, Princeton Theological Seminary, CN 821, Princeton, NJ 08542, USA

Wilson, Dr Henry (Church of South India), Lecturer/Director, 112/2 Nandidurg Extension, Bangalore 560 046, India

You, Ms Choon Ho (Presbyterian), Student, Im Heimgarten 1, Pfaffengrund, 6900 Heidelberg, Federal Republic of Germany

Organisers/Staff

Geense, Dr Adriaan (Reformed), Director/Lecturer, Ecumenical Institute, Bossey, 1298 Celigny, Switzerland

Moon, Dr Cyris (Presbyterian), Lecturer, Ecumenical Institute, Bossey, 1298 Celigny, Switzerland

Amirtham, Dr Samuel (Church of South India), Director/PTE, World Council of Churches, P.O. Box 66, 1211 Geneva 21, Switzerland

Martensen, Dr Daniel (Lutheran), Director/Lecturer, Washington Institute of Ecumenics, 487 Michigan Avenue N.E., Washington DC 20017, USA

Boyd, Dr Robin (Presbyterian), Director/Lecturer, Irish School of Ecumenics, Dublin Research Centre, Bea House, 20 Pembroke Park, Dublin 4, Ireland

Koch, Dr Margret (Old Catholic), Librarian, Ecumenical Institute, Bossey, 1298 Celigny, Switzerland

Ginglas-Poulet, Ms Roswitha (Roman Catholic), Interpreter, Ecumenical Institute, Bossey, 1298 Celigny, Switzerland

Pater, Ms Margaret (Methodist), Interpreter, Ecumenical Institute, Bossey, 1298 Celigny, Switzerland

Tatu, Ms Evelyne (Roman Catholic), Interpreter, Ecumenical Institute, Bossey, 1298 Celigny, Switzerland

Ray, Ms Sheila (Anglican), Administrative Assistant, Ecumenical Institute, Bossey, 1298 Celigny, Switzerland

Appendix 3
Contributors

Dr ALAN FALCONER teaches at the Irish School of Ecumenics, Dublin.

Rev. Dr PAUL A. CROW, Jr, is president of the Council on Christian Unity of the Disciples of Christ, USA.

Rev. Dr JOHN MBITI teaches Christianity and African religions in Bern University and serves as a pastor at Burgdorf, Switzerland.

Dr PROCORO VELASQUES is professor at the Methodist Institute for Higher Education in Sao Paulo, Brazil.

Dr T.V. PHILIP, from India, teaches church history in Brisbane, Australia.

Prof. Dr ADRIAAN GEENSE is director of the Ecumenical Institute, Bossey, Geneva.

Prof. DAVID KWANG-SUN SUH teaches at Ewha Women's University, Seoul, Korea.

Dr MARY HALL is lecturer at Selly Oak Colleges, Birmingham, England, and executive director of Birmingham Multifaith Resource Unit of the Foundation for Education and Citizenship.

Dr J. PAUL RAJASHEKAR is secretary for church and people of other faiths at the Lutheran World Federation, Geneva, Switzerland.

Rev. Dr CHARLES C. WEST teaches at Princeton Theological Seminary, New Jersey, USA. He was associate director of the Ecumenical Institute, Bossey, from 1956 to 1961.